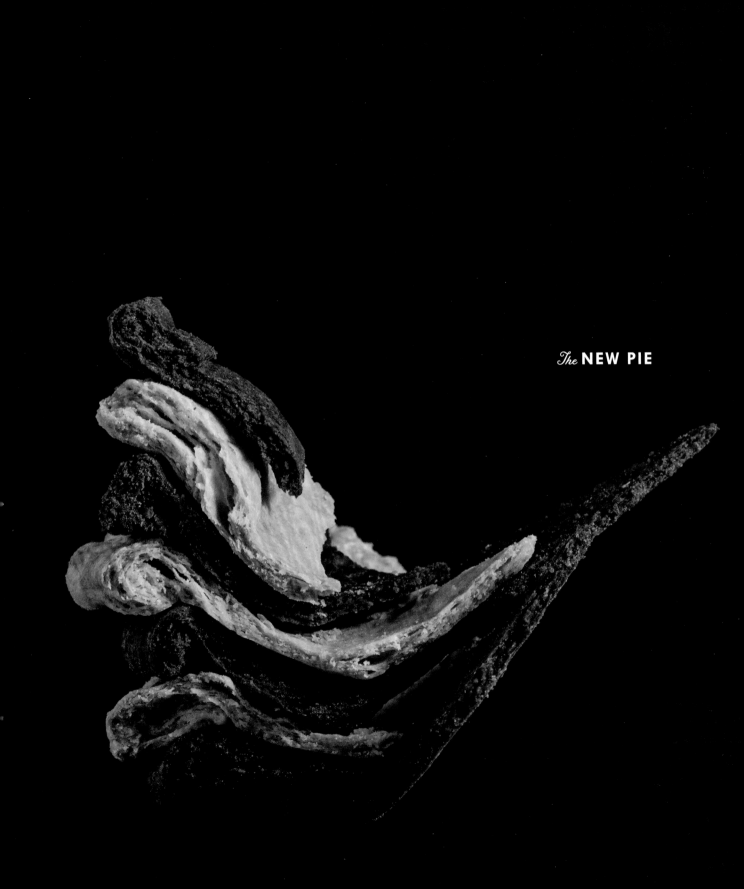

The NEW PIE

CLARKSON POTTER/PUBLISHERS
NEW YORK

The
NEW
PIE

MODERN TECHNIQUES
for the Classic AMERICAN DESSERT

by **CHRIS TAYLOR**
and **PAUL ARGUIN**

PHOTOGRAPHS BY
ANDREW THOMAS LEE

Published in the United States by Clarkson Potter/
Publishers, an imprint of the Crown Publishing Group,
a division of Penguin Random House LLC, New York.
crownpublishing.com
clarksonpotter.com

CLARKSON POTTER is a trademark and POTTER
with colophon is a registered trademark of
Penguin Random House LLC.

Library of Congress Cataloging-in-Publication Data
Names: Taylor, Chris, author. | Arguin, Paul M., author.
Title: The new pie : modern techniques for the classic
    American dessert / Chris Taylor and Paul Arguin.
Description: First edition. | New York : Clarkson Potter/
    Publishers, [2019]
Identifiers: LCCN 2018020959 | ISBN 9780525576440 |
    ISBN 9780525576457 (Ebook)
Subjects: LCSH: Pies. | Cooking—Technique. | LCGFT:
    Cookbooks.
Classification: LCC TX773 .T387 2019 | DDC
    641.86/52—dc23 LC record available at
    https://lccn.loc.gov/2018020959

ISBN 978-0-525-57644-0
Ebook ISBN 978-0-525-57645-7

Printed in China

Book and cover design by Mia Johnson
Cover photography by Andrew Thomas Lee

10 9 8 7 6 5 4 3 2 1

THIS IS DEDICATED
TO OUR MOMS,
WHO TAUGHT US HOW
TO BAKE WITH LOVE.

CONTENTS

1
The New
PIE CRUSTS

2
The New
CREAM PIES

3
The New
FRUIT PIES

4
The New
NUT PIES

IN THE WORLD OF BAKING, THE GOOD NEWS IS EVERYONE KNOWS PIE.

The bad news is *everyone knows pie,* and it's often the same pie: blueberry, cherry, apple, lemon meringue, and banana cream. We understand (we do!)—pie is a comfort food, and there is comfort found in traditional recipes that have lovingly passed hands through the generations. However, we are not traditional pie bakers. Two married doctors living in the South, we have won hundreds of awards for our baking, including the National Pie Championships title of 2017. Pies have become our greatest creative outlet. We have created, entered, and won (and lost!) pie contests with flavors that, while not new to the world, are certainly not traditional. Pies inspired by flavors like pineapple upside-down cake, bubble gum, breakfast cereal, and roasted beet and goat cheese are examples of how we transform unique flavors into pies that stand out against the backdrop of traditional rustic versions. Modern flavors and techniques are at the heart of who we are as pie bakers, and these fresh and fun ideas are what this cookbook is about. While we are passionate about the tradition of pie, and enjoy the flavors and techniques beloved by generations of pie makers, we don't believe that pie should be confined to what pie has always been.

In 2011, we entered Pie Squared, our first pie contest. It was in Dahlonega, a small town about an hour north of Atlanta. It's difficult to recall why we were even drawn to this particular contest. Sure, we loved to bake, and at this point in our lives, we had

both baked plenty of cakes and cookies, but in all honesty, we probably had not made more than ten pies *total* between us. Maybe we were drawn to the homespun novelty of a small-town pie contest. Maybe we realized that the contest was only a few miles away from our favorite outlet mall with the Williams-Sonoma store. Who can say? Regardless, we decided to each enter a pie and, well, make a day of it.

We decided not to compete against each other (a practice we still follow), so Paul entered a savory pie, and Chris entered a dessert pie. After strategizing, we decided that Chris would go the traditional route with a more classically flavored pie showcasing strawberries and lemon, while Paul went a more unconventional direction with a fiery-spiced beef pie with a simple top crust. We loaded our pies into the trunk of Paul's little Miata and headed north. Arriving at the community center just off the typical southern town square, we felt a bit out of place. The room was packed with locals providing directions on a first-name basis to friends and neighbors who they had probably known for years. "Sweet pies go over there by Helen;" and "Judging? I don't know, ask Bill if he knows when the results will be announced." After nervously dropping off our pies for judging (and feeling like complete interlopers in this tight-knit community event), we took a leisurely walk through the town. As it happens, there was confusion about when the winners would be announced, and by the time we got back to the venue, names and winners were already being called. We were still across the street when we heard a white-haired woman with a deep southern drawl call out, "In first place, with his Summer Strawberry Pie, Chris Taylor!" Chris had WON first place! He darted over to the stage to collect his ribbon and certificate.

As he smiled for his photo and felt the silkiness of the blue ribbon, he remembers thinking, "Is this woman a Paula Deen impersonator? Did she just happen to look like her, or was she hired for the event?" Anyway, one of us had won our first pie contest. Paul's beef pie with Scotch Bonnet peppers, patterned after a recipe from his childhood in the Virgin Islands, lost to a traditional chicken pot pie. We debated extensively whether it was a failure of design (was hot pepper wrong for this crowd?) or execution (the winning chicken pot pie was served piping hot in a chafing dish). Later on, we agreed on two things: It was definitely a Paula Deen impersonator, and we liked winning. A lot. And we liked doing it together.

In fact, baking was what brought us together as a couple. We had been introduced long distance by a mutual friend who thought we were so much alike we just *had* to meet. With Paul in Atlanta and Chris still finishing his PhD in Pittsburgh, a traditional in-person date was not possible. After our introductions, and learning we each enjoyed baking, we decided for our first date we ought to do something special. The sole cookbook common to both of our collections was *The Cake Bible* by Rose Levy Beranbaum. We decided to bake Rose's Scarlet Empress bombe, a daring achievement—a freestanding Bavarian custard molded in a half-sphere and covered with jellyroll slices filled with homemade raspberry preserves. We shared the adventure of making the bombe over an hours-long telephone date, disconnecting only when the whirs of our stand mixers were too loud for conversation. But this baking typified what would come to be our shared baking style—bold, unafraid to try something new, and often untraditional.

Chris eventually moved to Georgia and we began entering local baking competitions and state fairs, and we were quite successful at it. In 2013, we discovered the American Pie Council National Pie Championships and entered for the first time. Though we came away empty-handed that first year, the joy of developing pie recipes became a true passion. The National Pie Championships encouraged creativity, and we unmoored ourselves from traditional pie-baking methods and began exploring and creating new and exciting flavors and techniques—many that you'll see in this book. By the time we finally earned our coveted Best of Show Award in the Amateur Division at the 2017 National Pie Championships, we had entered into dozens of competitions and won hundreds of ribbons. We were even featured in the *New York Times* (along with our winning Checkerboard Peanut Butter Pie) in their food section—a major coup!

Married, and together more than nine years after our first date, we are still baking—and still winning. So far, we have earned more than 500 awards for baking pies, cakes, cookies, and breads at county and state fairs, as well as pies both at local contests and nationally. While our approach is novel, we offer plenty of detailed, foolproof instructions on how to build these pies. In addition to being bakers, we are scientists—each of us with doctorates in our fields—and scientists appreciate meticulous attention to details. Some recipes may look daunting, but we wrote this book so that our step-by-step instructions, peppered with a bit of wisdom and humor, can provide pie bakers of all levels with the knowledge they need to successfully create new and novel pie creations that will wow friends and family alike. They might even impress a pie-contest judge or two.

How to Use This Book

Whenever you get a new cookbook, you should spend a little time getting to know it. To start figuring a cookbook out, flip first to the recipes section. Go page by page, mostly looking at the pretty pictures and glancing lightly at the ingredient lists. This is going to create your general impression of the book and whet your appetite for the recipes you want to try first. Now go back to the beginning and read through the book. In addition to some fun stories, you will learn some vital information that we hope will improve your chances for success with the recipes in this book, and can also make you a better baker in general.

WEIGHT A MINUTE . . .

As you review our cookbook, one of the first things you'll note is that we give you a few different options for measuring your ingredients: by volume and by weight, in both standard and metric values. We provide these options so that everyone will be able to make these pies, regardless of their preferences for measuring ingredients. Is one method better than the other? Actually, yes. Weighing ingredients on a digital scale is better, for so many reasons. The first is accuracy. If you tell ten different people to measure out a cup of flour, you will likely end up with ten different amounts. Depending on how densely packed the grains of flour are, you can end up with either more or less flour than you intend. That error rate is compounded with each time an ingredient is imprecisely measured. Another example is irregularly shaped and sized items like chopped nuts. Larger chunks of nuts will create more air gaps in the measuring cup, resulting in fewer nuts per cup than nuts chopped uniformly smaller. Additionally, our recipes are developed using weight-based measurements, and there are some ingredients that just cannot be easily converted to convenient volume-based amounts. This can result in measurements like "1 cup plus 2 teaspoons" because that is the closest volume-based amount to the weight of the ingredient. In the "Essential Ingredients" section (page 12), we provide some tips for minimizing these errors and measuring ingredients accurately, but there is no question that with the use of a scale, you can correctly measure the proper amount of the ingredients every time.

The second reason for weighing ingredients is convenience. When measuring ingredients by weight you can often measure out the ingredient directly into your mixing bowls or saucepans. It may not sound like much of a timesaver, but in a busy kitchen, efficiency matters. You will see that we weigh our liquid ingredients, too. Be careful: liquid measurements in this book are based on weight, not volume. For example, 1 cup of whole milk equals 8 fluid ounces by volume but weighs 8.5 ounces by weight. We prefer the weight measurement. Finally, measuring by weight is cleaner. Measuring without additional cups and spoons means that those items don't have to be washed later. This is particularly enjoyable for recipes that use sticky ingredients like honey and molasses. Have we convinced you yet?

SEEING STARS

You'll also notice that we have included a star rating system in this book. All recipes include our rating of three factors that should be considered when baking the pie: ingredients, equipment, and construction. Each factor is graded on a scale of one to three stars as follows:

INGREDIENTS

★   All ingredients should be easy to find in an average grocery store

★★   The recipe has some unusual ingredients that may require going to a specialty store

★★★   The recipe has some very unusual ingredients that may need to be ordered online

EQUIPMENT

★   Requires only standard items used in a kitchen equipped for baking

★★   Uses unusual pieces of kitchen equipment that are found in most kitchen stores

★★★   Needs specialized equipment that the adventurous baker will be excited to use

CONSTRUCTION

★   Easy to make

★★   Requires a bit more effort

★★★   One of our more complex pies that is entirely doable if you follow the directions

These star ratings are not designed to scare you off! We thought you should know at a glance which pies take a little more time or effort to make or to find ingredients. These are not foolproof ratings. Depending on your baking experience, you may find some two-star pies very easy to assemble. Your grocery store might not stock all the one-star ingredients. These are general ratings to give you an idea of availability of ingredients and techniques—your mileage may vary.

For those of you up to the extra challenge, keep an eye out for the Blue Ribbon Bonus tips throughout the book. Those finishing touches will make your pie creations worthy of a shiny new blue ribbon—something we know a little bit about!

ESSENTIAL INGREDIENTS

As with any food, the quality of ingredients that go into making a pie greatly affects its flavor, aroma, and structure. There are some ingredients—granulated sugar, for example—where we are not brand loyal and will use whatever is on sale. But some specific brands or types of ingredients can make a big difference and result in a higher chance of success in making a perfect pie. For example, we use grade AA unsalted butter. Maybe you prefer to use higher-fat European-style butter. That's great, but know that our recipes are tested and developed with the ingredients described on the pages that follow; higher-fat European-style butter actually doesn't work as well in our crust because of the extra fat. If you'd like to try using different ingredients, please feel free to experiment! Experimenting is how we grow as pie makers—but remember, if you stick with our ingredients and methods, we know you'll make a delicious pie without having to wonder if your experiment will work. We have created a list of Sources (page 265) where you can find the less common ingredients used in the book.

Apple cider vinegar

Vinegar is an essential ingredient in our pie crusts. The acidity of the vinegar helps to deter gluten formation that can result in a tough crust. Don't worry—it does not change the taste of the finished crust. If you don't have apple cider vinegar, you can substitute white distilled vinegar.

Baking powder

You are probably used to using baking powder when making cakes or cookies. Baking powder is an essential ingredient in our pastry pie crusts. It provides a slight "puff" and contributes to flakiness. We wouldn't make our crusts without it! Remember to use only fresh baking powder. Baking powder loses its potency over time, so if your powder has expired or you've had it for more than a year, toss it and buy a new one.

Butter

Every pie in this book contains grade AA unsalted butter in one form or another. We don't use ultra or premium butters in our pies, so there's no need to shell out the big bucks for European-style high-fat butter. But when we say butter, we mean *butter*. Do not substitute margarine, anything made with oil, or products labeled as spreads. You need 100% real butter, and real butter does not contain oil or come in a tub. Our recipes are tested with unsalted butter; using salted butter might make your pie too salty.

Chocolate

Chocolate is a mixture of cocoa solids and cocoa butter extract from seeds (cocoa beans) of the cacao tree. Any chocolate-like product that doesn't contain both cocoa butter and cocoa solids is not chocolate (see "Candy Coating," page 13).

UNSWEETENED CHOCOLATE. Without any added sugar, unsweetened chocolate, labeled and sold as 99% or 100% cacao, has a bitter taste that not many people would enjoy as a snack. In recipes, unsweetened chocolate can be used with other ingredients to create a deep chocolate flavor without any additional sweetness.

BITTERSWEET AND SEMISWEET CHOCOLATE. When sugar is added to chocolate during the manufacturing process, it can be sold as bittersweet or semisweet chocolate. There are no laws that define what makes a bittersweet different from a semisweet. For our recipes, when we refer to bittersweet chocolate, we use a chocolate with a 60–62% cacao content. For semisweet chocolate, we prefer chocolates with around a 50–55% cacao content. Our preferred chocolate brand is Ghirardelli. We enjoy the flavor and the thin bars are easy to chop for use in baking.

MILK CHOCOLATE. Milk chocolate is a sweet form of chocolate made with added sugar and milk solids to create a sweet, creamy treat. Milk chocolate does not set in the same way as semisweet, bittersweet, or unsweetened chocolates. Substituting milk chocolate for another type of chocolate might cause your pie filling to be too loose or even not set at all. Don't take the risk—it's not worth the tears!

CHOCOLATE CHIPS. For the most part, chocolate chips are very similar to bar chocolate, with some chips even containing added emulsifiers and fats other than cocoa butter to help them keep their shape after baking (like in your favorite chocolate chip cookies). Because of these additional ingredients, most chocolate chips do not have a flavor as intense as bar chocolate. For recipes where melted chocolate is specified, we highly recommend using bar chocolate.

WHITE CHOCOLATE. Yes, we know white chocolate is not a *real* chocolate because it contains no cacao solids. Yes, we know it is sweeter than regular chocolate. Guess what? We are absolutely fine with that. We find white chocolate to be a very versatile ingredient, especially in our cream pie bases, because the white chocolate creates a smooth texture that feels delightful on the tongue.

COCOA POWDER. Cocoa powder is the dried, ground cacao solids left after cocoa butter is extracted following the fermenting and drying of the cocoa beans. If the light reddish-brown cocoa powder is left as it is, at this point it can be packaged as natural cocoa powder. Cocoa powder can be processed further in an alkalization process called Dutching, during which the flavor of the chocolate deepens and some of the natural acidity of the cocoa powder is reduced. We prefer to use this Dutch-process cocoa powder in our recipes, as we enjoy its deep chocolate flavor. Black cocoa powder is a form of Dutch-process cocoa that is processed further to create a black powder with an intense chocolate flavor. If you can't find black cocoa (see Sources, page 265), you can substitute regular Dutch-process cocoa powder.

CANDY COATING, or confectionery coating, is a chocolate-like candy that does not contain cocoa butter. It can be found at most craft stores and candy-making supply shops, and typically comes in 1-inch discs and often in a variety of colors—unlike chocolate, which comes in either white or brown. We use candy coating to easily decorate some pies in a way that real chocolates cannot without the need for tempering, a process in which chocolate is melted and cooled to ensure that it sets hard and shiny. We use candy coating several times throughout the book, like when creating the edible spoons as part of the Saturday Morning Cartoon Cereal (page 231).

Confectionery lace

Confectionery lace is a relatively new product used mostly in cake decorating, but, yes, it can contribute a lacy effect to pies, too. There are several brands, such as SugarVeil, that are supplied as powders to be mixed with water. Other brands are sold as a premade paste. The icing is spread onto patterned silicone mats and dried either at room temperature or in a low oven to create sugar lace that can be cut with scissors and used to decorate cakes, cookies, and pies, like the Mocha Mystery on page 70.

Corn syrup

Corn syrup is a form of liquid sugar made from the starch in corn. In pie making, it provides some sweetness, makes some glazes look shinier, and prevents crystallization of other sugars. Not to be confused with high-fructose corn syrup, corn syrup is all glucose, whereas high-fructose corn syrup has about half of its glucose converted to fructose, another form of sugar that is sweeter. Depending on where you live in the world, glucose syrup or golden syrup can be substituted for corn syrup.

Dulce de leche

Dulce de leche is caramelized sweetened condensed milk that looks like a glossy and very spreadable peanut butter. It is sweet and creamy with a deep caramel taste, and we use it (usually the Nestlé brand) throughout this book. It is often found in cans right next to the sweetened condensed milk or in the Hispanic/international foods section in your grocery store.

Eggs

For recipes in this book, we recommended using grade A or AA large eggs.

Extracts and flavors

Flavor extracts are natural or artificial ingredients usually dissolved in alcohol. They provide a very convenient and highly concentrated way of introducing or augmenting a particular flavor.

VANILLA EXTRACT is an alcohol-based extraction of flavor and scent from the vanilla bean. We use only pure vanilla bean extract. We like vanilla made from beans from Mexico, Madagascar, or Tahiti best, but use whatever variety you find delicious. Do not use imitation vanilla extract. Some artificial vanillas have harsh aftertastes that are quite noticeable when used in uncooked applications like whipped cream.

For other flavors, our preferred brands and flavors are included within the recipe.

Flour

Flour is the soul of pie crust! For our crusts, we use all-purpose flour (our favorite brand is King Arthur). King Arthur unbleached all-purpose flour is slightly higher in protein (11.7%) than most other brands (which usually offer between 10 and 11% protein). A higher protein content means the flour can absorb a bit more water than another brand. Be careful, though; if you handle dough made with a higher-protein flour too much, it can easily become tough.

Scooping flour directly from a bin or bag can pack flour into a measuring cup and result in a cup of flour weighing nearly 20% more than flour spooned into a cup. While we always weigh flour to ensure consistency and exactness, if you prefer using measuring cups, this method works best with our recipes: First, use a spoon to lightly stir and fluff the flour in the bag or container; then, use a dry measuring cup to scoop out enough flour to fill the measuring cup; finally, use the flat spine of a butter knife or some other flat edge to sweep the top of the flour even with the rim of the cup. This scoop-and-sweep method should result in a 5-ounce (142-gram) cup of flour, which is what our recipes call for.

Food colors

Food color comes in several forms and can be used to tint everything from icing to pie crust.

LIQUID FOOD COLORS. Most people are familiar with liquid food colors that are added to color a frosting or batter drop by drop. Similar to liquid food colors are food airbrush colors—liquid food dyes that are used when airbrushing food. The water-like consistency allows the dye to be sprayed out of the airbrush without clogging. You can airbrush with liquid food colors, but food airbrush colors come in a wider range of shades. Airbrush food colors can be found in some cake-decorating and crafts stores or online in nearly any shop that sells cake or cookie-decorating equipment. For airbrushing designs on chocolate, use an alcohol-based airbrush paint. A water-based airbrush color will bead up, since the fat in chocolate and the water in the color won't mix.

SOFT-GEL FOOD PASTE COLORS are a little thicker than liquid food color with a consistency between heavy cream and honey. These colors are used when you want a more intense color but don't want to add so much liquid food color that it thins out the consistency of your food. We use soft-gel food paste colors for royal icing. Because royal icing is used in specific consistencies for piping and flooding surfaces, if you wanted a bright blue color, you would have to add so much liquid food color that it would thin the icing down too much to use. A few drops of soft-gel food paste color would add enough color without thinning out the icing too much. Soft-gel food paste colors come in bottles with dropper lids so color can be added one drop at a time. One notable exception is white food color. White soft-gel paste color is sometimes much thinner, with a thickness similar to a liquid food color.

Golden syrup

Golden syrup is another form of liquid sugar. As its name implies, it is golden in color and tastes of caramel. At the grocery store, it can usually be found either with corn syrup or in the international foods aisle. If you have trouble finding it, corn syrup can be substituted.

Liquor and liqueurs

Alcoholic beverages feature prominently in the The New Cocktail Pies chapter (page 165) of this book, but pop up in other chapters, too. With the renaissance of the cocktail, there has been an explosion of fun-flavored libations, so why not use them in pies as well? In most applications in this book, the components containing the liquor are cooked either on the stovetop or in the oven, which allows the majority of the alcohol to evaporate.

Piping gel

Piping gel is corn syrup with additional ingredients including cornstarch. It is not an attractive food—think thick and gloppy like a colorless, flavorless canned pie filling. Used in small quantities, however, it is a great way to easily stabilize whipped cream, allowing a whipped cream–topped pie to stay perky for at least a full day or two, whereas whipped cream without piping gel will begin to soften and weep after a few hours.

Salt

Salt brings out the flavors of berries, deepens the flavors of chocolate, and ensures that a finished pie is flavorful and not "flat" or bland. When a recipe calls for a pinch of salt, we mean a two-finger pinch. In other words, use your thumb and index finger to pinch a portion of salt from a bowl of salt.

For most recipes in this book, we use table salt. You can use plain or iodized salt—your choice. We usually use plain (without iodine), as some people with sensitive palates can detect a bitter flavor from iodized salt. A few recipes also use kosher salt, a coarse-grain salt with no iodine. If a recipe calls for kosher salt, use a coarse kosher salt like Morton.

Soda syrups

SodaStream is an appliance that allows you to make seltzer or flavored carbonated sodas at home. Because they are so concentrated, we use the flavor syrups (like root beer in the Fizzy Root Beer Float on page 83) to add a great amount of flavor to pies. If you can't find SodaStream syrups (the brand we created and tested our recipes with), you can try substituting other flavored syrups like those used to flavor coffee drinks.

Sugars

We use several different types of sugar in this book. Most commonly we use regular white granulated sugar. While sugar's main role is to provide sweetness, it also promotes browning, contributes to flavors other than just basic sweetness (like caramel), and adds to the structure of some of the pie elements, such as the sugar crust on the top of a pecan pie and the brown sugar meringue on the King Fluffernutter (page 89). We also call for light brown, dark brown, and the really dark brown muscovado sugar that all add both moisture and varying degrees of molasses flavor to recipes. Dark brown sugar can be used as a substitute for the muscovado, but the flavor won't be as intense. Maple sugar, as you might expect, tastes maple-y. We specify exactly which sugar to use in each recipe, along with recommendations for substitutions when applicable. Confectioners' sugar, also known as powdered sugar, is simply regular white sugar that is finely ground

to a powder with a bit of cornstarch added to reduce clumping. Try not to go out on a limb and substitute things like honey or Splenda in place of actual sugar. Those other sweeteners may not perform all the functions that the sugar does in the recipe.

Thickeners

A thickener is any substance that is added to a liquid for the purpose of giving it more body. Small amounts of a thickener can change the mouthfeel of a liquid, while large amounts can convert a liquid to a solid, sliceable substance. Most thickeners usually need to be dissolved in the liquid and then heated to a specific temperature to activate the thickening agent. That process causes the thickener to form linkages, converting the mixture into a gel. The fillings used in our pies are thickened with a variety of substances, including eggs, gelatin, and starches.

CORNSTARCH is exactly what you think it is—a corn-based starch. It is used to thicken cooked mixtures, including the dairy-based pastry creams used in several of our cream pies. Cornstarch should be dissolved in a cold liquid that is then brought to a boil. Allowing the mixture to briefly boil ensures that that cornstarch is fully hydrated and will thicken the mixture properly. Cornstarch-thickened components don't freeze well because the item becomes grainy when thawed.

TAPIOCA is a starch produced from the cassava plant. We use two different forms of tapioca: tapioca starch and Minute Tapioca. Tapioca starch is a very fine powder that thickens at a lower temperature than cornstarch, creates a clearer gel, and doesn't interfere with flavor as much as cornstarch (which can mute flavor). On the downside, liquids thickened with tapioca starch can take on a rather slippery and unpleasant mouthfeel. We find that a 50/50 mixture of tapioca starch and cornstarch offers the best of both worlds—good flavor and an appealing mouthfeel.

The other formulation of tapioca we use is Minute Tapioca by Kraft. This type of tapioca has been precooked and dried as small granules. It dissolves easily and thickens quickly. A tip we learned from *Cook's Illustrated* is to grind the quick-cooking tapioca in a coffee grinder before adding it to a pie filling. This will make the hydrated granules of thickener less noticeable in the filling. We usually grind a whole box as soon as we buy it and store it in a jar so that it is conveniently ready to use in pies. The measurements in our recipes are for the already ground quick-cooking tapioca.

UNFLAVORED GELATIN comes in two forms: powder and sheets. For recipes in this book, we use unflavored powdered gelatin, such as Knox, available at nearly every supermarket in America. Gelatin sheets are often harder to find and come in a variety of strengths. Both are treated the same way: Add powder or sheets to a small amount of cold liquid (usually water) and allow the gelatin to hydrate for a few minutes before adding to a hot mixture to fully dissolve. Gelatin should never be boiled, regardless of whether it's in powdered or sheet form, because overheating will weaken its ability to set properly.

XANTHAN GUM. Don't let the chemical-y sounding name scare you off. Xanthan gum is a sugar fermentation by-product with many uses. You've probably seen it in the ingredient list of many different types of commercially prepared foods. By itself it is a weak thickener, usually added to give a creamier mouthfeel to liquids. Most grocery stores carry xanthan gum in the baking aisle near the baking powder and cornstarch or in the gluten-free or natural baking section, if your market has one.

DREADED SUBSTITUTIONS

Okay, let's get real. Blindly substituting ingredients in baking is something we are very passionate about. We dislike it. Strongly. *Very strongly.* Baking is a science. Successful baking relies on specific ingredients in specific amounts reacting with each other to create chemical reactions that result in something delicious. There are some ingredients in a pie that are there for flavor, some that are there because they add to structure, and most are for both. It's important to understand how a recipe works before seeking to change it. Remember—changing a recipe will mean that you will be conducting a science experiment and, like any science experiment, there is a chance for failure.

The internet is filled with comments from angry bakers who substituted ingredients and were left with a sad, inedible pile of steaming hot garbage. Some of those angry bakers like to blame the recipe (and the recipe writer!). Unfortunately, we (as recipe writers) can't imagine every iteration of an ingredient that could be substituted for another. Our recipes are what are in this book, complete with our specific ingredients and specialty equipment. They are written and tested and provided in this book in the hope that bakers will follow and enjoy them.

When you decide to make one of our pies, please follow the instructions as we wrote them in the recipe and use the ingredients in the amounts that we specified. If you make substitutions or follow a different method, then you are not using our recipe—you are using yours. Experimenting is great (and we encourage it!). If you have an idea for a flavor variation or a substitution, then by all means, give it a shot! However, if that substitution or new technique leaves you with a disaster, please don't blame us.

EQUIPMENT

There are definitely some tools that will make your pie-making life easier (and maybe even more fun). If you are unfamiliar with some of the tools we mention in a recipe, or not sure which ones to use, this section walks you through everything you need to know. We apply the science of modern kitchen technology and gadgets, from sous vide cooking blueberries and apples to make juicy, perfect fruit pies to using airbrushes to create beautiful crust designs that move beyond lattice and crimping. The great news is that these tools are not tremendously pricey, and they are becoming even more affordable all the time and, as a result, more mainstream as well.

Bench scrapers

A bench scraper is a simple rectangle of metal or plastic that can be used to release dough stuck to a work surface or clean up flour or sticky bits from a counter. They are particularly helpful and very inexpensive.

Cake/pie portion marker

This is a plastic tool designed for bakers to help cut round cake layers into equal-sized wedges. For pie purposes, it can be used to help divide a pie into equal slices or to help mark slices for the placement of whipped cream or other decorations. It can also be used to emboss the dough for a top crust with a sunburst pattern.

Cake turntable

Cake turntables are nothing more than lazy Susans—a round surface that spins. The best ones are also elevated with a surface that sits about 4 inches high. We use turntables to spin a pie when crimping the pie crust edge. We also use one to help smooth a creamy filling or to spread whipped cream over the top of a pie with an offset spatula. It's an indulgent addition to the pie enthusiast's tool kit.

Embossing mats

For several of our pies, we use tools to emboss a shape or pattern into the crust before baking. Most often, we use large silicone embossing or texture mats (usually marketed to cake decorators who emboss rolled fondant for adorning a cake). These mats are usually thicker than silicone baking mats and have deep pattern details that don't disappear during baking. We have also had success using smaller plastic texture mats (designed for texturing modeling clay); you can find them near the clay sculpting and modeling tools at crafts stores.

Flour shaker

The flour shaker allows for a fine dusting of flour to be added to a surface pre–dough rolling. Adding too much flour to the work surface to roll dough can cause a pie crust to become dry. We like shakers with about a 1- to 1½-cup capacity fitted with a removable fine-mesh screen.

Food processor

The food processor is our favorite way to make pie dough (see page 39). We prefer a model with about a 10- to 14-cup capacity so it can hold enough to successfully make a double batch of dough. When you make as many pies as we do, sometimes you don't have time to make them one at a time!

Immersion circulator and water bath

An immersion circulator is a device that heats water to a specific temperature and maintains the water at that exact temperature for the duration of the cooking process. This is the essential tool for sous vide cooking (see page 28). You can clamp the immersion circulator to the side of a large stockpot, plastic bin, or other large container big enough to contain the food (and water) being cooked. Refer to the instructions included with your immersion circulator to find out your machine's capacity.

Instant-read thermometer

An instant-read thermometer is critical to ensuring your custard pie filling is neither raw and runny nor overcooked and grainy. Throughout the book we provide specific target temperatures that ensure you either have gotten something hot enough or to prevent you from overcooking it. We guarantee it will become one of your most used kitchen tools.

Measuring cups

We prefer **LIQUID MEASURING CUPS** made from glass because they are microwave safe and can hold hot liquids without worry about their melting. Do not use liquid measuring cups when measuring dry ingredients like flour or sugar. You can't easily flatten the surface of a dry ingredient for a true measurement.

When measuring liquids, check the measurement at eye level. You will notice that the liquid in the glass appears to have a slight curve, known as the meniscus. For accurate measurement, measure liquids using the bottom of the meniscus curve. For the most accurate measurements, weigh your liquid ingredients on a scale! (See page 10.)

DRY MEASURING CUPS are designed for filling with dry ingredients, like flour or sugar, and then the top is scraped even for an accurate measurement. For the most accurate measurements, weigh your dry ingredients. (See page 10.)

Mixer

Because pies are relatively small compared to other desserts, we most often will use an electric hand mixer for our recipes. Don't get us wrong—we *loooove* our stand mixer, but for most recipes in this book, the volume of ingredients is too low for a stand mixer to effectively mix.

Offset spatula

These are great to help smooth all kinds of fillings into flat, even layers inside or on top of a pie. We like ones with a 4-inch flexible metal blade.

Pastry blender

A pastry blender is used for cutting fat into flour when making pie crust dough by hand. Choose one with a comfortable grip and sturdy metal blades. As with most kitchen tools, Oxo Good Grips makes a great one.

Pastry rings

Tart rings are ⅝-inch-tall metal rings with rolled edges on both the top and bottom. We use these to create even portions of certain pie components that are frozen, such as the topping in the Purple Plum (page 137). Other pastry rings or large cookie cutters can be useful for cutting

discs for the tops of pie like the pie dough cookie on The Chocolate Chocolate Chip (page 65).

Pie crust shields

Pie crust shields are rings that are designed to protect pie crusts from over-browning during baking. For most of our pie needs, a 10⅜-inch aluminum shield is our go-to. For large pie dishes, especially those with large rims, we have an 11½-inch aluminum shield. You can make your own by cutting out an 8-inch circle from a 12-inch square of heavy-duty aluminum foil. The circle cutout will allow your pie top to continue to bake while the foil edge protects the crust edge from over-browning or burning. We also use the pie crust shield to protect the edges of our crusts as we pour in fillings that can splash or drip.

Pie dams

These are great tools for storing a partially eaten pie. These are hinged wedges that are inserted into a finished pie after the first slices are removed to keep the cut surfaces of the pie covered and the filling in place.

Pie plates

Pie plates come in a variety of sizes and materials. In this book, we refer to pie plates of three different sizes; standard, deep-dish, and extra-large. Within those categories there is still a fair amount of variation, but if you are using a plate reasonably close in size to the one specified in the recipe, the filling should fit in there nicely. Before describing the plates, let's review the basic anatomy of a pie plate so that we are all measuring our plates in the same way. Pie plates all have a flat circular bottom and sloped sides. The technical name for this shape is a truncated cone, which means the diameter of the bottom of the pie will be smaller than the diameter of the top. Many pie plates will also have a flat or ruffled lip on top. Thus, the top also has two diameters: the top external diameter (going from the outside edge of the lip all the way across to the other outside edge) and the top internal diameter (which does not include the lip). *Aaack! Why does this sound like high school geometry all of a sudden?* We want to make sure you use a correctly sized pie dish. That's all. Pie dishes with a lip are useful for

Pie Dam   Embossing Mat   Instant-Read Thermometer

creating a crimped or fluted edge with pastry crusts. Pie plates without a lip are better for crumb crusts.

The *standard* pie plates we use have a top internal diameter of 8¾ to 9 inches. They are between 1⅜ and 1½ inches tall and have a capacity for about 3 cups of filling.

The *deep-dish* pie plates we use have a top internal diameter of 9⅛ to 9⅝ inches. They are between 1¾ and 2 inches tall and have a capacity for about 5 cups of filling.

The *extra-large* pie plate used for the Strawberry Chocolate Cosmos (see page 244) has a top internal diameter of 12 inches, is 1½ inches tall, and has a capacity for about 8 cups of filling.

In addition to different sizes, pie plates also are made of different materials, including metal, ceramic, and oven-safe glass. These materials conduct and retain heat differently, so naturally you can expect your pies to cook differently in them. When blind-baking your crusts in these different pans for the first time, take a peek under the foil or parchment liner about 10 minutes before the expected time to assess for doneness. You may need to adjust the baking times for certain pie plates that conduct heat more or less efficiently. We prefer using oven-safe glass such as Pyrex pie plates and ceramic pie plates such as those by Emile Henry. They are also sturdy and scratch resistant. One additional advantage

to the glass plates is that you can see through them to check if your bottom crust is appropriately browned when you are getting ready to remove the pie from the oven.

Always be sure to handle these hot pie plates with a dry oven mitt or towel. Placing hot pans on a cold or wet surface can cause the glass plates to shatter, so always place the hot pie on a trivet, cooling rack, or hot mitt to protect it. The metal pie plates we use are nondisposable aluminum. Try not to use disposable aluminum pie plates, if you can avoid it. They are kind of flimsy and can lead to disasters, especially with some of the heavier pies.

Pie server

When slicing a pie, the temptation is to just slide the blade of the knife under the slice of pie to serve it. Sometimes this works. Sometimes the slice of pie cracks and slips off the skinny knife blade, forming a messy heap on your tablecloth. An angled pie server is wider and sturdier, increasing your chances of successfully transferring that slice of pie safely to the plate.

Pie weights

Pie weights are used to prevent a crust from slumping and shrinking during blind-baking. Some people use beans, uncooked rice, sugar, or even pennies, but our preferred

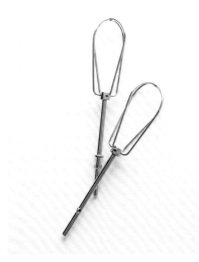

Electric Hand Mixer

Pie Crust Shields

Pie Weights

pie weights are just that—ceramic unglazed pie weights manufactured for baking. They cost more than beans, but they will last a lifetime. We recommend having at least 4 cups (2 pounds) of weights on hand for blind-baking standard pie crusts; 6 cups (3 pounds) for deep-dish crusts.

Piping bags, piping tips, and squeeze bottles
We have a selection of piping bags lying around the house and we think they are great tools to help make and decorate pies. We most often will use either standard 12- or 18-inch disposable plastic piping bags or tipless piping bags, which are very popular with cookie decorators. Either one is fine. If you don't want to purchase piping bags, you can most often use a plastic quart- or gallon-size zipper-top bag instead—just use scissors to snip off one of the corners in the bottom of the bag for piping. Depending on the task, we use a **PIPING TIP** with the piping bag, since tips make it easy to create a neat, even design. When a piping tip is needed, the recipe specifies the preferred tip to use.

For tasks like drizzling a glaze, we use **PLASTIC SQUEEZE BOTTLES**. These are inexpensive plastic bottles that hold around 1 cup of liquid or glaze and are similar to squeeze bottles used for ketchup or mustard.

Rolling pins
There are many different types of rolling pins. A ball-bearing rolling pin is the one that most people are familiar with. It is the pin used by most of our mothers and grandmothers with handles on either end and a center dowel that rolls. Straight or cylinder rolling pins are nothing but dowels of wood 1 to 2 inches thick, with no handles or moving parts. French, tapered rolling pins are thicker in the center with tapered ends. This type of pin is particularly good for keeping dough in a circle shape when rolling.

Rolling pin spacers
A perfect pie crust is one that is evenly baked, and even baking requires a crust that is the same thickness throughout. We use dough spacers to make sure every inch of our dough is rolled to our preferred thickness of ⅛ inch. We use "spacers" as a generic term because there are several tools that can be used to accomplish an even roll—like rolling pin rings that slip on to the end of a rolling pin and keep the pin ⅛ inch above the rolling surface. This ensures that the dough can never be thicker than the height of the ring. Slats of wood or plastic can perform the same task. The slats are placed at the left and right edges of the rolling surface and the rolling pin rests on the slats, ensuring even thickness. We prefer the rings to the slats

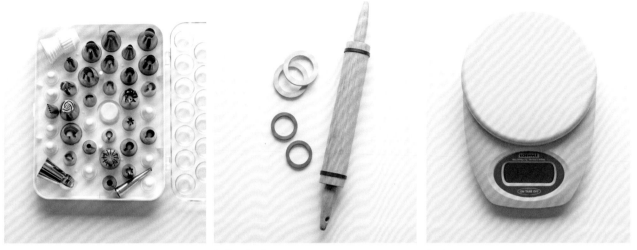

Piping Tips   Rolling Pin Spacers   Scale

because the rolling pin can be used in any direction with the rings. The slats can only be used in one direction unless they are repositioned. Rings or slats are usually sold in sets that allow for rolling a variety of thicknesses, usually from ⅟₁₆ to ½ inch. Note that spacers don't work with tapered-style rolling pins.

Scale

For the modern pie baker, digital scales are where it's at. If you want reliably repeatable results, precision matters. Measuring cups are great for convenience, but what they make up for in expediency, they lose in accuracy—a 1-cup dry measuring cup can be off by 2 tablespoons! If you multiply that for the nearly 3 cups of flour needed for a double-crust pie dough, your final dough could be short of more than ¼ cup of flour—and that could make for a disastrously wet dough that bakes up tough and shrinks more than it should. In this book, when we indicate a weight for an ingredient, that means we strongly recommend that you weigh the ingredient rather than use a measuring cup. Small amounts of ingredients, like spices or vanilla extract, can be measured with a measuring spoon, since most standard digital scales are not accurate enough for such small amounts.

Silicone pastry molds

A few pies in this book call for silicone pastry molds. These molds come in a variety of shapes and sizes and are good for molding pie components into fun and interesting shapes. They can come in simple shapes like hemispheres or cubes, or as more complex shapes that come in sets with multiple coordinating shapes that can be used to create intricate pie showpieces.

Hemisphere molds are silicone pastry molds that are used to create half-sphere shapes. These molds are especially useful for creating bubbles or other spheres like those for The Double Bubble (page 250). The half-spheres can be placed together to create whole spheres.

Silicone rolling mat

A silicone rolling mat will change the way you roll pie dough. The mat is a large sheet, about 2 feet wide, with concentric circles printed on the surface. Because it's made from silicone, it is practically nonstick. You need only a light dusting of flour to successfully roll out a pie dough—usually no more than about 1 tablespoon per crust. The concentric circles give you a guide to help you keep your dough round as you roll and let you know when your dough circle is the correct diameter. We use it every time we roll pie

Silicone Pastry Molds

Silicone Rolling Mat

Stencils

dough. One caveat—do not cut anything on your silicone mat. It is easily cut, and even the dull blade of a metal pizza cutter can shred it (we know, we've done it).

Stencils

For those of us who are not great artists with steady hands, stencils allow us to pretend that we are. Stencils are designs (both simple and intricate) made of food-grade plastic that come in innumerable patterns. Depending on the pie, dry ingredients like confectioners' sugar or cocoa can be sprinkled on top of the stencil to create a desired pattern. Stencils can also be used with an airbrush, usually on smaller components of the pie like garnishes. An airbrush stencil holder comes in handy for these tasks.

Tuile mold

This is yet another kitchen tool that Chris bought for its actual purpose (making super-thin and crisp tuile cookies) that Paul has repurposed for pie. It is a sheet of plastic about ¹⁄₁₆ inch thick with patterns cut out of it. We use it as a mold to make a decorative garnish for one of the pies. If you already own one, here is an opportunity to get another use out of it. You can also make your own by cutting a shape out of an old plastic lid.

Vacuum sealer

A vacuum sealer is a small electric kitchen appliance used for long-term food storage that removes the air from the inside of a plastic bag and then seals the bag shut using heat. One of the most popular vacuum sealer brands in the United States is FoodSaver. It is particularly useful for sous vide cooking (see note on page 28) because it allows you to get a reliable seal on the bag of food that is being placed in the water bath (you don't want water leaking into your bag or the food leaking out during the cooking process). Also, because most of the air is removed during the vacuum-sealing process, it is easier to immerse in the water. If you do not have a vacuum sealer, you can place food in heavy-duty zipper-top plastic bags and remove air by slowly dipping the filled bag into a water bath but keeping the top of the bag open above the surface. The water on the outside of the bag forces the air inside out. With the air removed and the bag is still in the water, you can seal the zipper top. If you use this method for sous vide cooking, be sure to clip the top of the bag to the side of the container using something like a binder clip to stop the top of the bag from floating around and falling into the water, which could cause water to leak into the zipper top. For sous vide cooking, we prefer the vacuum-sealed bags to zipper-top bags because the latter have a tendency to leak.

TECHNIQUES

Throughout this book we import techniques from the land of cake and cookie decorating to create beautiful designs and constructions in an effort to enhance the beloved tradition that is pie baking. You may already be familiar with how to do some of these, but some may be new to you. Consider this a primer on it all.

Coloring crusts

Coloring pie dough is a modern way to introduce color into what is often a plain-looking pie element. One way to color pie dough involves adding food color to the water used to make the dough. While the raw dough takes color nicely, baking colored dough is another matter entirely since the colors just don't hold up; browning will always occur in a well-baked crust.

For better results, we use a decorating airbrush (see page 266). Using liquid food colors developed for airbrushes (see page 15), you can dye a pie crust *after* baking, thereby allowing the colors to remain vibrant. Food airbrush colors come in a wide variety of shades, including bolds, pastels, and even metallic sheens like gold, silver, and copper. Even though we use water-based food airbrush colors, they do not soak in and moisten the crust because the colors are applied in thin even layers, allowing the moisture to evaporate before soaking into the crust.

It can take some time to become familiar with an airbrush. Chris left his in the box for eight months after buying it because he was so intimidated by it (now he uses it all the time). We provide a basic how-to for airbrushing a crust, but also there are loads of videos online that can help you learn to use one or troubleshoot problems with (and clean) your airbrush.

Before you begin, familiarize yourself with how your airbrush works (read that manual!). To airbrush a crust, remove the fully baked but not-yet-filled pie crust from the pie pan and place on two layers of paper towels (the towels act as a cushion to protect your delicate flaky crust from breaking). If you have lightly sprayed your pie pan and baked your crust fully until it's golden brown, the crust should easily release and come out in one piece. Removing the crust ensures that the airbrush color

doesn't go all over the side of the pan and create a mess of color running onto your work surface.

Using a liquid airbrush food color, add about 5 drops of color to the hopper of the airbrush. Gently apply light coats of color all over the crust edge (there's no need to color the inside of the crust because that will be covered by your delicious filling). Depending on the degree of color you want to achieve, you may need multiple coats of color. Refill the airbrush gun with color as needed. It's very important that you slowly build up the color, coat after coat. If you try to saturate an area with too much color all at once, you will end up with uneven blobs of color and maybe even a soggy crust. When applied lightly and gently in a series of coats, your pie crust will stay beautifully flaky and will not become wet from the airbrush color.

You can airbrush your pie crust with any type of airbrush color. We most often use standard colors, but metallic sheens like gold and silver can also be used. In fact, we suggest a gold or silver crust for our Lovey Dovey (page 241).

If you are intimidated by an airbrush or don't want to spend the money on one, you can also use canned food color spray. These cans are available at many crafts stores in the baking and cake decorating section as a substitute for airbrushing. Use the same techniques with the canned color as with the airbrush: Slowly build up color with light, even coverage and multiple coats of color. One brand of canned color spray, Wilton Color Mist, comes in a range of colors, including metallic sheens, and provides a good coverage, as well. Depending on how deeply you want to color your pie crust, each can of food color spray will color at least three pies.

Crimping crusts

The top edge of the crust serves a couple of purposes. It anchors the pie dough to the top of the plate, helping the pie to maintain shape during baking. For double-crust pies, the crimped edge creates a tight seal, preventing the filling from oozing out during baking. This crimped edge can be finished in innumerable ways, either quite simply or elaborately decorated. For the pies in this book, we give you creative license to crimp and finish the edges as we have done them in the photos, or to add your own flair. The edge can be finished simply by shaving the extra dough off with

a sharp knife pressed against the outer edge of the pie plate. As you trim it away, the edge of the dough will stick to the outer edge of the pie plate. When it bakes, the flaky layers of pastry will be visible in the cut edge. The edge can also be finished by folding or rolling the outer ½ inch of dough under itself and pressing it against the lip of the pie plate. This rolled edge can be left unadorned, pressed decoratively with the tines of a fork, the back edge of a knife, tip of a spoon, or even a texture roller or fancy fondant-decorating tool (see page 27), if you have one (a shell tool is particularly cool). A classic fluted edge can be made by pressing your knuckles or fingertips along the edge, creating a regular pattern of peaks and valleys. Finally, plunger-style pastry, small cookie, or fondant cutters, or even the wide end of a piping tip, can be used on thinly rolled pie dough to make ½- to 1-inch dough shapes that can be applied to the crust edge. These appliqués can either be pressed onto pie dough or glued on with a bit of egg wash.

Egg washes

Another way to add color to a crust is through the use of egg washes. Egg washes that are brushed on the top crust can add more than just shine. An egg wash made of yolk mixed with milk or heavy cream will become a rich brown color when baked. Gel food coloring can be added to egg white or egg yolk like tempera paints; yolk-based washes are quite vibrant while the egg white washes are subtler. Different washes can be used depending on the desired effect. If using a colored wash on a busy embossed top crust pattern, freeze the dough before the wash is applied to the embossed dough. Then, when the egg wash is brushed on the dough, the excess wash can be wiped off the surface because the pooled wash in the embossed pattern usually freezes before the wash on the surface of the dough (which would have obscured the design). If using an egg wash on the edge of a blind-baked crust, make sure that the foil or parchment containing the pie weights is not pressed against the egg-washed areas—it may stick when baking.

Embossing pie dough

Embossing the dough allows for the introduction of color and pattern to the top crust of a pie. Fondant texture mats and tools (see page 18) and plunger-style cookie cutters can be used to indent patterns into the dough. Once that patterned dough is chilled, an egg wash is applied; the egg wash pools into the indented areas so that when the dough is baked, the pattern remains.

The simplest type of dough embossing can be done with a **SPRING-LOADED PLUNGER-STYLE COOKIE CUTTER**. The idea is to cut out the shape from the dough by pressing on the edges of the cutter. Then press down on the plunger to emboss the surface of the dough with the design. The plunger can also be used to help release the dough from the cutter if it has gotten stuck there. These little pie crust cookies can then be arranged along the edge of the pie, across the surface of the filling, or glued to the surface of a pie crust with a bit of extra egg wash. If your design involves layering these items, be sure to roll the dough a bit thinner (¹⁄₁₆ inch, if possible) before embossing; otherwise, the layers of dough may not be fully baked by the time the rest of the pie is ready to come out of the oven.

More impressive crust designs can be achieved with **IMPRESSION MATS** made from flexible silicone or rigid plastic with the pattern molded onto one side (page 22). If you want to emboss an entire top crust, you'll need to find a mat with a diameter at least as large as the surface of your pie. Likewise, for embossing dough for a lattice-topped pie, the texture mat must be at least as long as your lattice strips. To use an impression mat, roll out the top crust as you normally would (if you are not using a silicone rolling mat, transfer the rolled dough onto a piece of parchment or roll it on parchment to begin with). Brush the embossing surface of the mat with a light dusting of flour and lay the mat on top of the dough. Using a non-tapered rolling pin, apply even pressure onto the mat, pressing it into the dough. Now slide the mat/parchment, dough, and impression mat onto something flat, like a large cutting board or baking sheet, and place it in the refrigerator or freezer. Once the dough has firmed up (takes about 10 minutes), the impression mat can be lifted off the dough, revealing the embossed pattern. The dough should remain chilled until assembling the filled pie. Once assembled, you will likely have to return the pie to the refrigerator or freezer before the embossed pattern has chilled sufficiently to be firm to the touch. If you apply the egg wash when the dough is too soft, you may accidentally brush away the embossed pattern.

Even items not typically used in the kitchen can be adapted to pie making! **TEXTURE ROLLERS**, designed to imprint patterns on clays, work great on pie dough, too. Rollers come in various widths and can be used to texture just a crust edge, lattice strips, or the entire top crust. We prefer to use those made of wood or resin because they can be cleaned easily.

GUMPASTE AND FONDANT TOOLS are small plastic hand tools with different-shaped tips, sold individually or sometimes in sets. A Dresden tool or leaf-veining tool can be used to reinforce some of the shallow impressions made by your impression mat or to make your own designs in the dough. If you are a skilled artist with a steady hand, these tools will allow you to carve your own designs into the dough surface. Other tools, like the shell tool, are useful for creating fun patterns in the crimped edges of the pie instead of just using your fingertips or the tines of a fork.

Lattice and cutout tops

Lattice tops are a beautiful way to introduce texture and pattern to a top crust. The lattice strips can all be equal in size, or you can have some wide strips and some skinny strips to create a more modern variation on the lattice weave. To make a lattice-top crust, follow the directions in the recipe to roll and cut the dough strips to the specified width and place in the refrigerator to chill. After the strips are firm and pliable like a leather belt, but not so soft that the dough stretches, remove the pan from the refrigerator. If the dough is a little too firm, that's okay—it will warm up quickly once it's removed from the refrigerator.

On a parchment-lined sheet pan, lay down about seven 1-inch strips about ¼ inch apart to create a set of parallel dough strips 10 inches across. This is enough to cover the top of the pie. Gently fold back the ends of every other dough strip to meet the other end, essentially folding it in half (do not crease the fold). Slide another strip of dough crosswise to the strips and lay it on top of the unfolded strips. Return the ends of the folded dough to their starting point. Fold back the other alternating strips of dough and place a second strip of dough ¼ inch away from and parallel to the strip just laid. Continue folding back alternating dough strips and inserting dough strips until the grid is fully woven.

An alternative to creating a lattice top is using small cookie or fondant cutters to cut out shapes from the top crust dough. Depending on the intricacy of the pattern, the best size for the cutters is less than 1 inch in length. Any shapes will work, but very narrow shapes might trap the dough and be difficult to clean.

Melting chocolate and candy coating

We prefer melting chocolate and candy coating in the microwave because it is fast and efficient. Add finely chopped chocolate to a microwave safe bowl that is large enough to accommodate the chocolate and some stirring. Heat the chocolate or coating at medium (50%) power, stopping to stir every 30 seconds. When the chocolate is 80 to 90% melted, remove the bowl from the microwave and continue stirring, allowing the heat of the bowl to melt any remaining pieces.

The classic way to melt chocolate is in a bowl over a water bath on the stove. This is a fine method, but it takes much longer and requires using a pot. In a medium saucepan, bring 1 inch of water to a simmer over medium heat. Add finely chopped chocolate to a heat-safe bowl and set the bowl on the saucepan so the bowl rests on the lip of the saucepan but does not touch the water beneath it. Making sure to keep the water at a simmer, stir the chocolate frequently with a rubber spatula until the chocolate is melted, 10 to 20 minutes, depending on the amount of chocolate to melt. The chocolate will seize and become clumpy if it comes into contact with the steam or any splashed water, and you will have to start over with more chocolate.

Sous vide

Sous vide is a precision cooking method that uses heated water maintained at a specific preset temperature to cook food. Because of its ability to reliably and easily achieve exact results every time, this method is a core technique in the modernist cooking movement and is now, with immersion circulators available online for $100 or less, becoming more mainstream. Common uses for this technique have been poaching eggs at a precise temperature to ensure that the yolk is the exact degree of runniness preferred or cooking steaks to the exact level of doneness desired, then just finishing them on the grill or in a blazing-hot pan to get a perfect sear. The food is usually sealed inside a plastic bag, which both protects it from the water and allows as much surface area of the food as possible to be in contact with the heat. Use bags designated as food-safe, microwave-safe, or specifically BPA-free to avoid concerns about cooking in plastic. Because the water is being maintained at the desired end temperature, the food cannot be overcooked. If the temperature of the water is 150°F, the food can never exceed that temperature, even if it is left in the water bath too long. This degree of control over the cooking process can be quite useful. Heating foods to a certain temperature for a certain amount of time can kill bacteria (i.e., pasteurization) and cause proteins to break down, pectin to gel, and particles to dissolve into solution. These are all things we do to food on the stovetop or in the oven. With the sous vide technique, you can achieve spectacular results every time. We use sous vide for pie fillings because fruits can be cooked to the point where they no longer taste raw but still maintain their structure.

The pie fillings in this book that are cooked with the sous vide method are all fruits. Some of the recipes involve separating the fruit solids from the released juices after cooking and then thickening those juices to get reintroduced to the filling in a second step. This helps take the guesswork about adding the right amount of thickener out of the equation. Some batches of fruit are juicier than others—this depends on the level of ripeness, seasonality, variety, and other uncontrollable factors. By using the sous vide technique, not only can you assure that the fruits are cooked perfectly but you can also pre-thicken the fruit juices before the pie is baked. Think about that for a moment. Using traditional pie methods, the thickener hydrates and gels inside the pie while the crust is baking. You don't know exactly how much liquid will be released from the fruits, so you may or may not have added the right amount of thickener. Likewise, in order to activate all that thickener, the liquids in the pie need to reach the boiling point throughout the pie. The result is often a messy pie with fruit syrup oozing out on top of the crust and dripping out of the pie. This is not only messy but you are also losing that delicious fruit gel that we all want to keep inside the pie. The sous vide technique ensures that the amount of fruit liquid in the pie will be appropriately thickened and will stay neatly in the pie, right where you want it.

Depending on the density of the fruit and how successful you were at evacuating the air from the bag, sometimes these bags of fruit have a tendency to float. You can attach weights to the bag using metal binder clips or place something heavy on top of the bag to keep it immersed in the water bath. We find that a heavy metal roasting rack works well to keep bags of fruit under the water. Keep a kitchen towel to catch drips and a pair of tongs handy when retrieving the bags from the hot water bath.

Toasting coconut

Spread the premeasured amount of shredded coconut onto a half sheet pan and place it in a 350°F oven on the middle rack. After about 4 minutes, give the coconut a stir with a rubber spatula, making sure that the pieces on the edge get moved to the middle, and return the pan to the oven. You'll start to smell the delicious aroma of toasted coconut. Check the coconut every minute or so, stirring if needed, until the coconut has transformed from bright white to lightly suntanned. It takes about a total of 7 minutes to toast 1 to 2 cups of coconut. Don't let it get dark brown; it will start to taste bitter.

Toasting nuts

Nuts that are raw or just blanched to remove their skins definitely improve in flavor when toasted (see page 154). You'll note that the few times we use raw nuts in a recipe are when the nuts are exposed on the surface of the pie and will toast as the pie is baked. Toasting nuts separately can be done in two ways. For large amounts of nuts (1 or more cups), we use the same technique as described for toasting coconut. About 7 minutes at 350°F seems to be the right amount of heat to toast most nuts. For light-colored nuts like blanched almonds, you will see a noticeable change in color when the nuts are properly toasted. For darker nuts like pecans, the color change is subtler and you will have to rely more on the toasted nut aroma to know when you have achieved your goal. For smaller amounts of nuts, it is usually easier to just place them in a small skillet over medium heat on the stovetop. Every 30 seconds or so, swirl and flip the nuts in the pan until they start to smell toasty and/or are evenly and lightly browned.

STRANGER DANGER: *Baking in an Unfamiliar Oven*

You'd think that the middle rack of an oven preheated to 350°F the way it is at your house would be the same everywhere else. Sadly, that is not always the case. Some ovens are very good at maintaining a near constant temperature. Others will oscillate above and below the target temperature so that on average it is accurate, but not very precise. There is also variability in ventilation, and humidity and even the closeness of the oven walls can affect how things will bake.

Where possible, we try to provide visual cues in addition to the time and temperature so that baking times can be adjusted to account for these variables.

After baking in your own oven for a while, you become used to its quirks and idiosyncrasies and have learned to adjust. But what do you do when you are asked to bake the Thanksgiving pies at someone else's house? We suggest you take the oven for a bit of a test drive first. Check the accuracy of the oven using an oven thermometer. Simply place the thermometer in the middle of the oven and heat the oven to a desired temperature. When the oven chimes to indicate that it has preheated, check the oven thermometer. It likely will not have reached the target yet. Most ovens need a bit more time than the standard preheat to reach and hold the target temperature. Keep rechecking every 10 to 15 minutes. After about 30 minutes,

the oven thermometer should be telling you what the actual temperature of the oven is. You hope it matches the target temperature you set. If not, you now know that you'll need to make some adjustments when you bake. You can also check the oven for hot spots by placing slices of white sandwich bread directly on the oven racks to toast. Ideally, all the slices will brown evenly at the same time. If you notice that one of the slices in the back burned while the slices in the front remain pale, you may want to try to keep your pie away from that hot spot in the back and rotate the pie a bit more frequently than you normally would. Feel free to snack on the toast now or incorporate it into the Thanksgiving stuffing. Nothing goes to waste.

The NEW PIE CRUSTS

THE SECRET *for* THE PERFECT PIE CRUST

We're here to tell you that making perfect pie crust can be as easy as pie. Before revealing our secrets, though, let's discuss what pie crust *is*. One of the reasons it may be so difficult for bakers to achieve the perfect pie crust is that there is a surprising lack of agreement about what makes the perfect pie crust. It is a combination of flour, fat, and water that, when baked, forms flaky layers of a crisp pastry that holds a filling. The pastry needs to be strong enough to provide structure to the pie yet still embody all those qualities that make pie so wonderful. Many people have imprinted an early memory of pie like their own grandmother's pie crust, regardless of what that actually was. It may have actually been perfect or may objectively have been too thick, too thin, tough, mealy, soggy, or even chewy. But it was made with love and associated with happy memories, so it has become their personal gold standard. Anything dissimilar by definition must be some kind of failure. In *The Man Who Ate Everything*, author Jeffrey Steingarten gives one of the best descriptions of the characteristics of the perfect pie crust we have come across; and in his opinion, it must be seven things all at once: flaky, airy, light, tender, crisp, well-browned, and good tasting. We agree, and that is the standard we are guiding you toward.

Another factor contributing to widespread pie crust anxiety disorder is imprecision. Many pie crust recipes seem to have been written by friendly folk giving directions on a country road. "Yeah, just head up yonder for a piece and turn left by the funny-looking tree—you'll know it when you see it." Those instructions might take you where you want to go some of the time, but if you are not in the mood for an adventure involving deadends, backtracking, and getting completely lost in the woods with an inedible pie, some exact, step-by-step instructions with precise numbers might be more comforting. There is a myth that pie dough is a fickle product that on some days can require dramatically different amounts of flour or water. When the home baker is routinely advised to add between 2 and 6 tablespoons of water based on a judgment of the look or the feel of the dough, it is no wonder that baker is scared off. The fact is, most of us are fortunate enough to live in temperate climates and reside in houses with access to heating and cooling when needed. As such, the temperature and humidity in our kitchens vary over a relatively narrow range. When we are comfortable (not too hot or sweaty), usually our baking ingredients are comfortable, too. Their physical properties will not be changing on you from day to day. Be reassured that you are standing on solid ground. If you follow the instructions in our recipes that measure out exact amounts of ingredients (just like you would follow the driving directions of your GPS), we can reliably guide you right to the heart of Pietown. In order to have that level of precision, our preferred method of measuring ingredients for making pie crusts is by weight (ounces or grams) and NOT by volume (cups). So please, weigh your ingredients.

Please do that.

Really, we mean it.

It's really worth it, and it can make such a change in how reliable a recipe can be (rest assured, we provide volume measurements as well, because we know there will be some who really want to make these pies, but either do not own a kitchen scale or are for some reason averse to using one). We are often told that baking, unlike cooking, is an exact science and that rigidity can be off-putting for some. Many believe there is only one right way to do it, and it must be done that way every time. Not true. There are many roads leading to Rome and many ways to make a great pie crust. In *Baking and Pastry: Mastering the Art and Craft,* the chefs at the Culinary Institute of America explain that pie crust, in its most basic form, is just three ingredients combined in a ratio of three parts flour, two parts fat, such as butter, shortening, or lard, and one part liquid (usually water). Pretty simple! As long as that formula is at the core of a recipe, it is possible to produce a viable pie crust using many different methods. In addition to those three core ingredients, we include a bit of sugar (for flavor and browning), salt (for flavor), baking powder (for browning and lightness), and vinegar (for tenderness). We think our pie crust recipes are the bees' knees; however, if you already have a reliable pie crust recipe that you love, you can use it when making our pies. You won't hurt our feelings.

Finally, in addition to the flour, fat, and water, pie crust has two additional, less tangible ingredients: temperature and time. The temperature of the ingredients really does matter. In our recipes, we specify cold butter and cold water when assembling the dough. Warm ingredients will be more difficult to handle and will result in an inferior crust that can be tough. If your kitchen is warmer than you'd like, you can even place the flour and bowl in the freezer beforehand to beat the heat. Likewise, time is a really important factor. Dominique Ansel even describes time as an essential ingredient in his book, *The Secret Recipes.* Work quickly when mixing the dough and rolling out the dough so that the ingredients do not have the opportunity to warm up. Also, be sure to give the dough sufficient time to rest in the refrigerator so that the flour will be fully hydrated, the proteins in the dough will have relaxed, and the butter will have firmed up.

In this section, we provide several sets of ingredients for making different quantities of pie crust. After trying all-shortening, all-butter, high-fat European-style butter, and lard, we have arrived at a combination of mostly butter with some shortening as our preferred fats for pie crust (see "A Word About Lard and Shortening" on page 42). Taste an all-butter crust and an all-shortening crust side by side, and I think you'll agree that the flavor of the butter crust is far superior. However, replacing a bit of the butter with some shortening produces a dough that is a bit softer, easier to roll, and a little more flexible when handling than an all-butter crust. These recipes are scaled for a standard single pie crust, a standard double crust, a deep-dish single crust, and a deep-dish double crust, depending on how much you may need (see page 19 for more on pie plates). The pie recipes later in the book specify the appropriate option or options for a particular pie.

We also provide a choice of method for making those crusts. While the ingredients stay the same, you can make a pie crust completely by hand with a pastry blender or use a food processor. As you read through the instructions, you'll find that both methods follow essentially the same steps. Dry ingredients are combined, fat is dispersed into them, followed by the liquid. Finally, sufficient friction is applied to just get everything to stick together. We use both of these methods with very similar results. Making pie dough by hand takes more time than with a food processor, so you may want to use the faster option. You may not own a food processor, or you may simply prefer getting your hands in the dough and making your crust old-school! Just pick the method with which you feel most comfortable and follow the steps. Remember—easy as pie!

PASTRY *Pie Crusts*

These are the recipes for our standard flaky pie crusts. Each crust has a delightful buttery flavor and bakes up deliciously crisp and flaky (the methods instructing on how to make the dough are pages 38–39). We have provided four different sets of ingredients for the convenience of making the right amount of dough for either single- or double-crust pies in either standard or deep-dish pie plates. Each version of our standard crust, including the gingerbread variation, can be made by hand or with a food processor using the method that follows. You can double these recipes to make twice as many crusts at one time. The crusts will keep, wrapped, in the refrigerator for up to three days. Wrapped in plastic and placed in a freezer-safe zipper-top storage bag, they can be frozen for up to six months.

STANDARD SINGLE CRUST

Here is the quintessentially crisp, flaky, golden brown, and delicious pie crust.

MAKES ABOUT 12 OUNCES OF DOUGH FOR A 9 BY 1½-INCH STANDARD PIE PLATE

INGREDIENT	VOLUME	WEIGHT (STANDARD)	WEIGHT (METRIC)
All-purpose flour	1 cup plus 3 tablespoons	6 ounces	170 grams
Sugar	1¼ teaspoons		
Salt	½ teaspoon		
Baking powder	⅛ teaspoon		
Vegetable shortening	3 tablespoons plus 2 teaspoons	1.5 ounces	43 grams
Cold unsalted butter, cut into 6 pieces	6 tablespoons	3 ounces	85 grams
Apple cider vinegar	1 teaspoon		
Cold water (see instructions, pages 38 or 39)	3 tablespoons	1.6 ounces	45 grams

STANDARD DOUBLE CRUST

MAKES ABOUT 22 OUNCES OF DOUGH (12-OUNCE BOTTOM CRUST AND 10-OUNCE TOP CRUST) FOR A 9 BY 1½-INCH STANDARD PIE PLATE

INGREDIENT	VOLUME	WEIGHT (STANDARD)	WEIGHT (METRIC)
All-purpose flour	2 cups plus 3 tablespoons	11 ounces	312 grams
Sugar	2¼ teaspoons		
Salt	¾ teaspoon		
Baking powder	⅛ teaspoon		
Vegetable shortening	6 tablespoons	2.5 ounces	71 grams
Cold unsalted butter, cut into 11 pieces	11 tablespoons	5.5 ounces	156 grams
Apple cider vinegar	1½ teaspoons		
Cold water (see instructions, pages 38 or 39)	5½ tablespoons	3 ounces	85 grams

DEEP-DISH SINGLE CRUST

MAKES ABOUT 15 OUNCES OF DOUGH FOR A DEEP-DISH PIE (ABOUT 9½ BY 2 INCHES)

INGREDIENT	VOLUME	WEIGHT (STANDARD)	WEIGHT (METRIC)
All-purpose flour	1½ cups	7.5 ounces	213 grams
Sugar	1½ teaspoons		
Salt	½ teaspoon		
Baking powder	⅛ teaspoon		
Vegetable shortening	3 tablespoons plus 2 teaspoons	1.5 ounces	43 grams
Cold unsalted butter, cut into 8 pieces	8 tablespoons	4 ounces	113 grams
Apple cider vinegar	1 teaspoon		
Cold water (see instructions, pages 38 or 39)	3 tablespoons plus 2 teaspoons	2 ounces	57 grams

DEEP-DISH DOUBLE CRUST

MAKES ABOUT 26 OUNCES OF DOUGH (15-OUNCE BOTTOM CRUST AND 11-OUNCE TOP CRUST) FOR A DEEP-DISH PIE (ABOUT 9½ BY 2 INCHES)

INGREDIENT	VOLUME	WEIGHT (STANDARD)	WEIGHT (METRIC)
All-purpose flour	2⅔ cups	13 ounces	369 grams
Sugar	2½ teaspoons		
Salt	¾ teaspoon		
Baking powder	¼ teaspoon		
Vegetable shortening	6 tablespoons	2.5 ounces	71 grams
Cold unsalted butter, cut into 14 pieces	14 tablespoons	7 ounces	198 grams
Apple cider vinegar	1½ teaspoons		
Cold water (see instructions, pages 38 or 39)	6½ tablespoons	3.5 ounces	99 grams

GINGERBREAD CRUST

This variation on the standard flaky pastry adds the molasses flavor of dark muscovado sugar and some warm spices to complement the flavors of the Gingerbread Cashew pie (page 162). This could also be a delicious alternative for the Dulce de Pumpkin (page 192), Spiced Apple Cider (page 97), or West Indies Wedding pies (page 123). Follow the same method as for the basic pie crust on page 38, substituting the muscovado sugar for plain sugar, and adding the cinnamon and ginger to the flour along with the salt and baking powder. Dark brown sugar can be used in place of the muscovado (see "Sugars," page 16).

MAKES ABOUT 22 OUNCES OF DOUGH (15-OUNCE BOTTOM CRUST AND 7 OUNCES FOR DECORATING THE TOP) FOR A DEEP-DISH PIE (ABOUT 9½ BY 2 INCHES, OR FOR A STANDARD 9 BY 1½-INCH DOUBLE-CRUST PIE)

INGREDIENT	VOLUME	WEIGHT (STANDARD)	WEIGHT (METRIC)
All-purpose flour	2 cups plus 3 tablespoons	11 ounces	312 grams
Dark muscovado sugar, lightly packed	2¼ teaspoons		
Salt	¾ teaspoon		
Baking powder	⅛ teaspoon		
Ground cinnamon	¼ teaspoon		
Ground ginger	¼ teaspoon		
Vegetable shortening	6 tablespoons	2.5 ounces	71 grams
Cold unsalted butter, cut into 11 pieces	11 tablespoons	5.5 ounces	156 grams
Apple cider vinegar	1½ teaspoons		
Cold water (see instructions, pages 38 or 39)	5½ tablespoons	3 ounces	85 grams

BAKING POWDER'S POWER *to Puff Pie Pastry*

You will notice that we use a small bit of baking powder in our pie crusts. While it may seem unusual, we are certainly not the first to do so. You can find it included in recipes in Louis P. De Gouy's *The Pie Book* and *The Pie and Pastry Bible* by Rose Levy Beranbaum (where we saw it first). Rose explains, and we agree, that baking powder gives pie crust lift and aerates it. We find that the slight "puff" from the baking powder makes the crust feel lighter and, actually, flakier. Note, however, that some baking powders made with aluminum-containing salts might leave an unpleasant aftertaste, so it's best to stick to aluminum-free baking powders.

MAKING
PIE DOUGH
by Hand

This is how many mothers and grandmothers (like ours) made pie dough.

1. Measure the flour, sugar, salt, and baking powder directly into a large mixing bowl. Stir the contents with your pastry blender or a whisk until well mixed.

2. Add the shortening and butter pieces to the flour. Cut the fat into the flour by pressing on the pieces of butter with the tines of the pastry blender, which will break them into smaller pieces and incorporate them into the flour. Keep moving and pressing the pastry blender around the bowl until all the larger chunks of butter and shortening have become much smaller. Reach into the flour with your hand and lift out a small handful of the mixture. Use your thumb and fingertips to press and smear any pieces of fat that are larger than ¼ inch across. Repeat until all the larger pieces of fat have been broken up and mostly incorporated into the flour. You should still be able to see small (less than ¼-inch) flecks of butter in the flour.

3. If measuring all ingredients by volume (measuring cups), simply combine the vinegar with the cold water and drizzle all of the liquid over the flour. If using a scale, place a liquid measuring cup with a spout on the scale and tare (zero out) the scale to subtract the weight of the measuring cup. Add the measured amount of vinegar to the cup (do not re-tare the scale); now add the cold water to the vinegar so that the combined vinegar plus water equals the weight of cold water listed in the ingredients. Drizzle the liquid over the flour.

4. Using a rubber spatula, stir the mixture until the water seems to have been all absorbed. The dough will still appear loose and crumbly. Using either the rubber spatula or the heel of your hand, press the wetter pieces of dough into the drier pieces of dough against the sides of the bowl. Continue until all the drier portions seem moistened and have clumped into shaggy clusters.

5. Remove the dough pieces from the bowl and press them together into a 5- to 6-inch disc on a piece of plastic wrap. If making a double batch or a recipe for a double crust, divide the dough into 2 discs using the weights specified in the recipe.

6. Wrap the disc(s) in plastic wrap, and smooth the outer 1-inch-thick edge with your fingertips or by rolling the disc along the countertop. These smooth edges will make the dough easier to roll out in a circle. Refrigerate for at least 4 hours but preferably overnight.

7. To roll out the dough, see "Rolling Out Crusts" on page 42 or the directions in the pie recipe. If specified, blind-bake (page 47) the crust.

MAKING PIE DOUGH
Using a Food Processor

This has become our favorite method because it is faster, easier on the forearm muscles, and produces a crust that is identical to the one made by hand. If our grandmothers had had food processors, it would have been their favorite, too. Sometimes, the old ways are the best, but sometimes a change is welcomed. Yay for kitchen appliances!

1. Measure the flour, sugar, salt, and baking powder directly into the bowl of a food processor. Pulse the ingredients once or twice to combine them.

2. Scatter the shortening across the top of the flour mixture in three or four roughly equal nuggets. Pulse three to four times until the shortening seems to be evenly dispersed into the flour. If there are still large visible clumps, pulse one or two more times.

3. Scatter the butter pieces across the flour mixture, and pulse four or five times. At this point the flour should appear textured, like coarse cornmeal, with small (¼-inch) tidbits of butter flecked throughout. If not, pulse one or two more times.

4. If measuring all ingredients by volume (measuring cups), simply combine the vinegar with the cold water and drizzle all the liquid over the flour. If using a scale, place a liquid measuring cup with a spout on the scale and tare (zero out) the scale to subtract the weight of the measuring cup. Add the measured amount of vinegar to the cup (do not re-tare the scale); now add the cold water to the vinegar so that the combined vinegar plus water equals the weight of cold water listed in the ingredients. Drizzle the liquid over the flour in the food processor.

5. Using 1-second pulses, process the mixture until it transforms from dry and powdery and just begins to form into a large clump of cohesive dough, five to eight pulses. Stop pulsing once most of the dough is clumped together. The dough may look like pebbly curds of cottage cheese and there may be unincorporated flour in the bowl. That is what you want at this point. If you process the dough until it forms one large ball of dough and starts thwacking around in the food processor bowl, it will be overworked and bake up tough.

6. Transfer the dough and any remaining unincorporated flour to a smooth work surface (you can use a silicone rolling mat if you like, but we usually do this straight on the counter). To incorporate any loose flour, press and smear the flour across the work surface with the heel of your hand. Gather all of the dough and press it into a 5- to 6-inch disc about 1 inch thick. If making a double batch or a recipe for a double crust, divide the dough into 2 discs using the weights specified in the recipe.

7. Wrap the disc(s) in plastic wrap, and smooth the outer 1-inch-thick edge with your fingertips or by rolling the disc along the countertop. These smooth edges will make the dough easier to roll out in a circle. Refrigerate for at least 4 hours but preferably overnight.

8. To roll out the dough, see "Rolling Out Crusts" on page 42 or the directions in the pie recipe. If specified, blind-bake (page 47) the crust.

COCOA
Pastry Crust

MAKES ABOUT 15 OUNCES OF DOUGH FOR A 9 BY 1½-INCH STANDARD PIE PLATE OR A 9½ BY 2-INCH DEEP-DISH PIE PLATE. The recipe can be doubled and used for a double-crust pie.

This crust is used for several of the pies in this book, including the Pittsburgh Proud (page 81) and the Chocolate-Covered Cherry (page 129). Chocolate crusts can be tricky. The addition of cocoa powder affects the flavor, sweetness, browning, and gluten formation. This recipe works because we first combine the cocoa powder and confectioners' sugar with the shortening to form a paste, rather than adding them directly to the dry ingredients. We've found that the chocolate paste is more easily and evenly dispersed into the dry ingredients using a food processor rather than by hand so we are providing only one method for making it. Like the standard pastry crusts, you can double this recipe to make two crusts at one time. This dough will keep, wrapped, in the refrigerator for up to 3 days. Placed in a freezer-safe zipper-top storage bag, it can be frozen for up to 6 months.

1. Measure the flour, salt, and baking powder directly into the bowl of a food processor. Pulse the ingredients once or twice to combine them.

2. Place the shortening, confectioners' sugar, and cocoa into a separate small bowl. Using a small rubber spatula, smear the shortening into the powders, pressing against the sides and bottom of the bowl. Continue to work your way around the bowl until all the ingredients have been combined into a chocolatey paste. Using the small rubber spatula, divide the chocolatey paste into three or four roughly equal nuggets and add them to the flour mixture. Pulse three or four times (1-second pulses) until the chocolate seems to be evenly dispersed into the flour.

3. Add the butter to the flour and pulse four or five times. At this point the flour should appear slightly textured, like coarse cornmeal, with small bits of butter flecked throughout. If not, pulse one or two more times.

4. If measuring all ingredients by volume (measuring cups), simply combine the vanilla with the cold coffee and drizzle all the liquid over the flour. If using a scale, place a liquid measuring cup with a spout on the scale and tare (zero out) the scale to zero to subtract the weight of the measuring cup. Add the measured amount of vanilla to the cup (do not re-tare the scale); now add the cold coffee to the vanilla so that the combined vanilla plus coffee equals the weight for strongly brewed coffee listed in the ingredients. Drizzle the liquid over the flour in the food processor.

INGREDIENT	VOLUME	WEIGHT (STANDARD)	WEIGHT (METRIC)
All-purpose flour	1⅓ cups	6.75 ounces	191 grams
Salt	½ teaspoon		
Baking powder	⅛ teaspoon		
Vegetable shortening	2½ tablespoons	1 ounce	28 grams
Confectioners' sugar	¼ cup	1 ounce	28 grams
Dutch-process cocoa powder, either standard or black (see Sources, page 265)	¼ cup	0.75 ounce	21 grams
Cold unsalted butter, cut into 8 pieces	8 tablespoons	4 ounces	113 grams
Vanilla extract	1 teaspoon		
Strongly brewed coffee, cold (see Step 4)	3 tablespoons plus 2 teaspoons	2 ounces	57 grams

5   Using 1-second pulses, process the mixture until it transforms from dry and powdery into a large clump of cohesive dough, 8 to 15 pulses. Stop pulsing once most of the dough is clumped together.

6   Transfer the dough and any remaining unincorporated flour to a smooth work surface. To incorporate any loose flour, press and smear the flour across the work surface with the heel of your hand. Gather all the dough and press it into a 5- to 6-inch disc about 1 inch thick.

7   Wrap the disc(s) in plastic wrap, and smooth the outer 1-inch-thick edge with your fingertips or by rolling the disc along the countertop. These smooth edges will make the dough easier to roll out in a circle. Refrigerate for at least 4 hours but preferably overnight.

8   To roll out the dough, see "Rolling Out Crusts" (page 42) or the directions in the pie recipe. If specified, blind-bake (page 47) the crust.

Rolling Out
CRUSTS

As is the case with many aspects of life, the key to rolling out a crust is preparation. If you're an experienced pie maker, rolling out dough may seem intuitive. However, every now and then, everyone needs a good refresher on the basics. If you are already a skilled pie maker and feel comfortable rolling out pie dough using your own gadgets and tricks, please continue to do so. However, we will share our methods, and maybe some of these ideas will improve your dough-rolling experience or quell any fears you may have about rolling pie dough.

ROLL ON A FLAT SURFACE. Rolling out pie dough is best done on a large, smooth, flat surface that is relatively cool. Smooth kitchen counters work well, but try to avoid areas where the counter can heat up, such as near a dishwasher or next to a warm stove or oven. If you have a tiled countertop, that can make rolling pie dough difficult because of the texture. In that case, you can also use a dining room table, but the lower height of the table may make rolling the dough uncomfortable on your back.

USE A SILICONE ROLLING MAT. Paul used to always roll out dough directly on a floured countertop. When Chris first suggested that Paul try the silicone dough rolling mat (see page 22), Paul scoffed. "Isn't that for kids? Do I really need a mat to show me how to roll dough into the shape of a circle?" Then he tried it, and well, that was the end of the story—we are now both huge fans of silicone rolling mats. You use less flour, the dough is less likely to stick, and the concentric circles printed on the mat actually are quite helpful in ensuring that the dough is rolled out to the proper size. After you have found your flat, cool surface, place your silicone rolling mat on it and start assembling the rest of your tools.

HAVE YOUR TOOLS HANDY. We like to have all our tools in place within easy reach so we are not running all over the kitchen looking for things while the dough is getting warm waiting for us. The main tools we like to always have on hand are a flour shaker for dusting the

A WORD ABOUT LARD AND SHORTENING

We recognize that some people may not like the idea of using hydrogenated vegetable shortening because it is a manufactured product. There is a more natural alternative, which is leaf lard. Leaf lard is a smooth white to off-white substance rendered from the fat around the kidneys of a pig. It has a similar melting point as shortening and is regarded by many pie bakers to be a superior fat for making flaky pie crusts. Leaf lard, when properly rendered, has almost no pork flavor and is well suited to making crusts for both sweet and savory pies. We've used it by itself and mixed with butter, and agree that it works really well. So why do we still generally prefer the shortening? Depending on where you live, leaf lard may not be as readily available or as inexpensive as shortening, though some mail-order sources do exist. Also, depending on where you get it from, the quality and flavor of the lard may not be as consistent as shortening. We've had some batches start to taste a bit bacon-y (which is not always a bad thing). In general, the lard found on your average grocery store shelf is not leaf lard and will most likely have an assertive "piggy" taste. If you're not into pork-chop-and-strawberry pies, steer clear of the grocery store and seek out a source for high-quality leaf lard. Bottom line: If you want to make these pies but don't want to use shortening, go ahead and substitute an equal amount of leaf lard in its place. Vegetable shortening is just fine for us.

work surface, cooking spray, rolling pins (both a tapered French-style pin and an even-thickness dowel-style pin), dough thickness guides, a turntable, the pie plate, and a clean pair of scissors. You don't need all these things—just have whatever you like to use within arm's reach. Additional tools, like impression mats, cookie cutters, and fondant-decorating tools, should be at the ready if called for in making a specific pie.

READY TO ROLL. Spray a light layer of cooking spray over the inner surface of the pie plate. This provides some extra insurance that each slice is easily removed. Place the pie plate near the rolling mat, but not in the way. Remove the dough from the refrigerator and unwrap it. Dust the rolling mat, rolling pin, and both sides of the dough disc lightly with flour.

ROLL QUICKLY. You should not be rushing, but you want to work efficiently with the dough. Because our doughs are mostly butter, the doughs are hard and firm directly out of the refrigerator. The longer the dough is out of the refrigerator, the softer the butter gets, and the less flaky your final crust will be. Once you have started rolling out the dough, you will have a limited amount of time to complete the process. That time is mostly dependent on the temperature in your kitchen. When making pies in a warm kitchen, we start rolling the dough immediately after removing it from the refrigerator. In most other settings, you might want to wait 2 to 5 minutes for the butter in the dough to soften *slightly* before you start rolling. The dough should still be firm. The dough should begin to roll with slight pressure from the rolling pin. If the edge starts to crack, it is usually because the dough is too cold. Press the cracks together, stop rolling, and wait another minute before continuing.

ROLLING BASICS. Place the center of a tapered rolling pin in the middle of the disc of dough. Roll the rolling pin toward you, pressing slightly harder with your right hand than your left. Lift the disc of dough and spin it a quarter-turn counterclockwise (use a bench scraper, page 18, to help release the dough from the surface or mat if needed and re-flour your surface). If you start rolling when the dough is too cold or press too hard on the cold dough with the rolling pin, the edges of the disc can start to crack and split. If this happens, stop, press the cracked edges

back together, and smooth the edge. That process may be sufficient to warm the disc of dough slightly from the heat of your hand, or you may need to wait another minute before restarting. Continue rolling and spinning the dough in this manner for four quarter turns. Turn the dough over and continue rolling and spinning the dough. If you find the dough beginning to stick anywhere, dust the surface with a bit more flour. If you find the dough is sticking to the rolling pin, you can also sprinkle a light dusting of flour on the top of the dough, as well. By keeping the dough constantly moving by turning it, there is less chance the dough will stick and you are more likely to roll it into a circle shape. If you keep the dough in place, it may adhere to the rolling surface, and you won't realize it until it's time to lift the dough into the pie plate, and you might end up with an oddly shaped piece of dough that could prove to be a challenge to fit into a round pie plate. Don't worry if the edges of your pie dough become a little ragged as you roll; the edges get trimmed away once the dough is positioned in the pie plate. If at any point it becomes clear to you that the dough has become too warm and soft, you can transfer the dough on the silicone rolling mat into the refrigerator for a few minutes until it has firmed up a bit.

Once your dough is about 10 inches across, you can add ⅛-inch dough guides to help get the perfect, even ⅛-inch thickness we call for in our recipes (dough guides don't work on tapered rolling pins, so if you're using a French pin, you may choose to switch to a non-tapered dowel-style rolling pin or a standard ball-bearing pin at this point; see page 21). If you don't have dough guides, you can use these measurements to help steer you—once the dough has reached this size, it will be ⅛ inch thick.

For bottom crusts, the dough circles should measure:
• 13 inches in diameter for a standard 9 by 1½-inch pie plate
• 15 inches in diameter for a 9½ by 2-inch deep-dish pie plate
• 15 inches in diameter for a 12 by 1½-inch pie plate

For top crusts, the dough should be about 2 inches wider than the diameter of the top of the pie plate. For example, if your pie plate measures 10 inches from lip edge to lip edge, roll the dough to a 12-inch circle. These measurements should take into account the roughness in the dough's edge, and the fact that the rough edges will be trimmed away.

If there is a part of the circle that is less than the 13 or 15 inches specified, there may be a gap in your crust edge. You may have to patch this area later. Sometimes, to ensure all the dough bakes evenly, we roll the dough thinner than ⅛ inch, like when layering pieces on top of dough (such as lattice crusts with layered dough strips). Those directions will be included in the individual pie recipes. When the dough is at an even thickness, the size of the dough circle will vary depending on whether you are using a standard or deep-dish crust recipe.

TRANSFERRING THE DOUGH TO THE PIE PLATE. Place the rolling pin along the edge of the crust farthest from you. Using your fingertips, lift the edge of the crust onto the rolling pin and roll the pin toward yourself to wrap the dough loosely around the pin. Lift the dough and pin from the mat. Unroll the pin over the pie plate and allow the dough to settle in place so that equal amounts of dough are hanging over the edge all around. If you place the dough off-center, gently (gently!) reposition the dough using a very light touch. You do not want to stretch the dough at this point.

Using both hands, lift an edge of the dough and guide that portion down into the pie plate. The goal is to make sure that the dough is touching the surface of the pie plate all over—this is especially important where the bottom and sides of the pie plate meet. It should feel like you are draping a heavy piece of cloth into the pie plate. Try not to stretch

the dough—stretched dough will only shrink back to its original size in the oven and give you a sad, shrunken crust. Continue working your way around the pie plate, fitting the dough into the bottom and against the sides (a cake decorating turntable makes this process easier).

TRIMMING THE OVERHANG. Once the dough is flush against all of the inner surfaces of the pie plate, you should have about 1 inch of extra dough hanging over the edge of the pie plate. For a single-crust recipe, use the scissors to trim the extra dough to about ½ inch beyond the pie plate edge. Fold the edge of the pie crust underneath itself. The folded edge should be flush against the edge of the pie plate. Crimp the edges as desired with your fingertips, knuckles,

or using a decorative tool like the tines of a fork (see "Crimping Crusts," page 24).

These recipes err on the side of giving you a bit of breathing room in the form of extra dough, just in case your dough circle isn't exactly round or your edges are a little ragged. Keep these dough scraps on hand while you bake your crust in case you happen to end up with a tear or hole (see "Fixing Cracks, Rips, Tears, and Holes," page 46). You can save any leftover trimmings of dough well wrapped in plastic in the freezer. After thawing, they can be pressed together into a new disc of dough for another pie. The rerolled scraps will be a bit tougher than the original dough, but it won't go to waste.

FIXING CRACKS, RIPS, TEARS, AND HOLES: *The Pie Dough Spackle*

Sometimes life isn't fair. You may have accidentally stretched the dough too much when fitting it into the pie plate. Or you were trying to follow all the steps carefully but got distracted at the wrong moment and poked your finger through the pie dough. You tried to patch it before baking, but the patch did not hold during the blind-baking. Arrrgh—that can be very frustrating! These things happen. If you do notice any small cracks or holes, grab that wad of pie dough scraps you have been saving in the refrigerator. Pinch off a small piece of dough and carefully smear it into the crack like putty. Be mindful—the pie crust is still very hot. An offset spatula would be useful about now. Bake the crust for an additional 5 minutes. If the rest of the crust is already sufficiently baked, simply cover those parts with a pie crust shield or aluminum foil to prevent them from getting too dark while your patched area is baking.

Blind
BAKING

WHAT YOU NEED
- Cooking spray
- Pie weights (see page 20)
- 18-inch-square piece of aluminum foil

"Blind-baking" is the term for either partially or fully baking the dough for a single crust pie *before* the filling is added. Generally speaking, crusts for cream pies are fully blind-baked before being filled, while crusts for custards that require baking, like a pumpkin pie, are partially blind-baked to give them a head start on becoming crisp-golden, and then the filling is added usually while the crust is still hot. To blind-bake, the unbaked dough is lined with foil or parchment and then pie weights (see page 20) are added to keep the crust in place while it bakes to prevent slumping and shrinkage.

BAKING THE COCOA PASTRY CRUST

When baking the Cocoa Pastry Crust (page 40), the visual cues become a bit less helpful since the dark crust makes it harder to see when the dough transitions from raw to lightly browned or fully baked. In addition to the time and temperature instructions provided, you can lightly tap the crust with the pad of your finger to assess doneness. If the crust still seems wet and soft, you are not there yet. The finished crust will feel dry, crispy, and firm.

1. Roll the dough to the specified diameter for the pie plate you are using (see page 19). Remember that the target thickness for a bottom pie crust is ⅛ inch. Place the dough in the pie pan and crimp the edges as desired. Freeze the dough-lined pan for at least 20 minutes while preheating the oven to 350°F.

2. Lightly spray one side of an 18-inch piece of aluminum foil with cooking spray. Line the crust with the foil, sprayed side down. Fill the pan with pie weights. For standard pie plates, use 4 cups of pie weights. For deep-dish crusts, use 6 cups. Completely cover the edges of the crust with the foil.

FOR A PARTIALLY BLIND-BAKED CRUST, remove the pie from the oven when the edge is a light golden brown, 40 to 50 minutes. Lift out the pie weights using the corners of the foil. The goal is for the inside of the pie shell to be just beginning to brown. If the pie is too pale, return the crust to the oven without the weights and continue to bake, checking every 2 minutes or until the bottom is just beginning to turn light golden brown in spots. The pie will bake longer after the filling is added, so it should not be completely browned at this point. Partially blind-baked crusts are usually filled hot out of the oven, so keep that in mind when preparing the pie filling.

FOR A FULLY BLIND-BAKED AND COOLED CRUST, bake the crust until the edge is golden brown, 50 to 60 minutes, peeking under the edge of the foil to check for doneness. Remove the pie pan from the oven and lift out the pie weights using the corners of the parchment or foil. The goal is for the inside of the pie shell to be evenly golden brown—it should look like a finished crust. If the crust is still too pale, place it back into the oven without weights and continue to bake, checking every 2 minutes. Use a pie crust shield (see page 19) if you don't want the edges to brown any further. Cool the pie crust completely on a wire rack, about 1 hour.

CRUMB
Crusts

It is worth your while to become familiar with crumb crusts. These crusts are all made by grinding up existing items like cookies, nuts, or breakfast cereals to produce the crumbs that become your pie crust. They are faster and easier to make than pastry crusts, and especially good if you need a blind-baked crust but haven't *quite* mastered the pastry crust. Crumb crusts are also a great way to introduce additional flavors to a pie beyond the flavors possible with pastry crusts. We blind-bake all our crumb crusts before adding the fillings. We find that baked crumb crusts are more flavorful and hold together much better than those that are left raw.

You'll note that the underlying formulas for these crusts are all very similar: crumbs + butter + sugar. Does this mean that you can experiment with additional types of cookies, cereals, and even snacks like pretzels? Yes, you can! However, pay close attention to the amount of fat that is present in the experimental cookie. Items with a similar amount of fat per equal weight of serving listed on the nutritional label of a graham cracker should work in place of graham crackers. Items with higher fat content may slump when baking, requiring you to reduce the amount of butter in the recipe. If you don't feel like experimenting, don't. We've already done that and provided you with several delicious crumb crust recipes.

GRAHAM CRACKER CRUST

This is the classic graham cracker crust. You can substitute an equal weight of graham cracker crumbs for the whole crackers. If you're in the habit of using the store-bought premade graham cracker crusts, please stop. This crust is so much better and very easy to make.

MAKES ONE 9½ BY 2-INCH DEEP-DISH PIE CRUST

INGREDIENT	VOLUME	WEIGHT (STANDARD)	WEIGHT (METRIC)
Graham crackers, broken into several pieces	12 graham cracker sheets	6.85 ounces	194 grams
Unsalted butter, melted	6 tablespoons	3 ounces	85 grams
Sugar	2 tablespoons plus 2 teaspoons	1.2 ounces	33 grams
Salt	pinch		

1. In the bowl of a food processor, process the graham crackers until finely ground. If you do not have a food processor or just prefer to do it by hand, place the graham crackers in a plastic bag and crush them with your rolling pin until they have been reduced to fine crumbs. Pour the crumbs into a bowl and proceed with the recipe, stirring in the other ingredients by hand using a rubber spatula.

2. Pulse in the melted butter, sugar, and salt until the crumbs are moistened throughout, resembling wet sand. Transfer the crumb mixture to a 9½-inch deep-dish pie crust. We prefer the glass Pyrex pans with no lip (see "Equipment," page 19).

3. Using your fingers, spread the moistened crumbs evenly around the bottom and up the sides of the pie plate. Press the crumbs firmly so that they start to adhere all along the inner surface of the pie plate.

4. Find a sturdy cup or small bowl with smooth sides and bottom—a ⅓ cup dry measuring cup works well. Use the bottom and side of the cup to compact the crumbs into a smooth even layer. Pay special attention to the area where the sides and bottom of the pie plate meet.

5. When you think you have finished, carefully hold the pie plate up to the light and visually inspect it from several angles. Do this carefully (like, don't turn it upside down or anything!). If you're using a glass pie plate, lift up the pan and look through the bottom toward a light source. If you find thick or thin areas or even actual holes, this is your opportunity to correct your mistakes. Scrape off some crumbs from the thick area and move them to the thin. Compact and smooth crumbs with the cup.

6. When you are satisfied, start preheating the oven to 350°F, and place the crust in the freezer to chill for at least 10 minutes.

7. Bake the crust for 10 minutes on the middle rack. Depending on the pie recipe, the crust may need to be filled warm or cold.

COCOA GRAHAM CRACKER CRUST

This chocolate-flavored version of the graham cracker crust is so tasty! To make it, follow the Graham Cracker Crust recipe (page 48), substituting the light brown sugar for granulated sugar and adding the Dutch-process cocoa powder, espresso powder, and vanilla to the melted butter before pulsing it into the crumbs. The result is a chocolate crust that is packed with more chocolate flavor than you thought a graham cracker could have. Feel free to use chocolate graham crackers instead, for even more chocolate reinforcement.

MAKES ONE 9½ BY 2-INCH DEEP-DISH PIE CRUST

INGREDIENT	VOLUME	WEIGHT (STANDARD)	WEIGHT (METRIC)
Graham crackers, broken into several pieces	13 graham cracker sheets	7.4 ounces	209 grams
Unsalted butter, melted	6 tablespoons	3 ounces	85 grams
Dutch-process cocoa powder, sifted	¼ cup	0.75 ounce	21 grams
Instant espresso powder	½ teaspoon		
Vanilla extract	1 teaspoon		
Light brown sugar, lightly packed	¼ cup	1.75 ounces	50 grams
Salt	pinch		

NUT GRAHAM CRACKER CRUST

The addition of walnuts or pecans is a delicious complement to the traditional graham cracker crust. There is no need to toast the nuts first because they will cook while the crust bakes. Process the nuts with the sugar and salt until the mixture is fine, then add the graham crackers and proceed with the Graham Cracker Crust recipe (page 48).

MAKES ONE 9½ BY 2-INCH DEEP-DISH PIE CRUST

INGREDIENT	VOLUME	WEIGHT (STANDARD)	WEIGHT (METRIC)
Walnut or pecan halves	½ cup plus 1 tablespoon	2 ounces	57 grams
Sugar	3 tablespoons	1.3 ounces	37 grams
Salt	pinch		
Graham crackers, broken into several pieces	9 graham cracker sheets	5.1 ounces	144 grams
Unsalted butter, melted	4 tablespoons	2 ounces	57 grams

GLUTEN-FREE CRUMB CRUST

This is honestly one of our favorite crumb crusts; the fact that it's gluten-free is a happy by-product. The sweetness and nuttiness from the Cheerios and the almond flour make it absolutely fabulous. To make it, follow the instructions for the Graham Cracker Crust recipe (page 48), replacing the graham crackers with Honey Nut Cheerios and almond flour. This recipe uses no added salt.

MAKES ONE 9½ BY 2-INCH DEEP-DISH PIE CRUST

INGREDIENT	VOLUME	WEIGHT (STANDARD)	WEIGHT (METRIC)
Honey Nut Cheerios	3¾ cups	5 ounces	142 grams
Almond flour	⅓ cup	1 ounce	28 grams
Unsalted butter, melted	6 tablespoons	3 ounces	84 grams
Sugar	¼ cup	1.75 ounces	50 grams

ALPHA-BITS CEREAL CRUMB CRUST

Alpha-Bits is a slightly sweet multigrain cereal. The bits make a fun alternative to a graham cracker crust, especially if the flavor of graham crackers is too "loud" for a subtle pie filling, such as the Saturday Morning Cartoon Cereal (page 231). Follow the instructions for the Graham Cracker Crust (page 48), substituting Alpha-Bits cereal for the graham crackers.

MAKES ONE 9½ BY 2-INCH DEEP-DISH PIE CRUST

INGREDIENT	VOLUME	WEIGHT (STANDARD)	WEIGHT (METRIC)
Alpha-Bits cereal	4 cups	5 ounces	142 grams
Unsalted butter, melted	6 tablespoons	3 ounces	85 grams
Sugar	¼ cup	1.75 ounces	50 grams
Salt	pinch		

The NEW CREAM PIES

Oh, the luscious decadence of a cream pie! These cream pies are a cut above many of the instant pudding–based cream pies we had as children. Our cream pies are made with traditional techniques for pastry creams, custards, and mousses, along with modern flavors like Thai iced tea and root beer, to create spectacular pies that are modern and inspired but still as comforting as a slice of pie should be.

PB & J

WHAT YOU NEED
- Standard Single Crust (page 35), blind-baked and cooled in a standard 9-inch pie plate
- Piping bag (see page 21) fitted with an Ateco #802 or another ¼-inch round piping tip

The peanut butter and jelly sandwich is one of the best sandwiches ever created. *Ever.* While it's often relegated to the world of schoolchildren, we believe that there is no age limit to enjoying this simple, satisfying, and nostalgic treat. In this pie, we pair peanut butter with raspberry jam (our favorite PB & J combo), but any flavor of jam can be used. Stick to jam for this simple pie—jelly is too soft to cut well, and preserves are often too chunky.

1. Transfer the raspberry jam to the piping bag (see page 21).

2. MAKE THE PB & J CREAM: In a small bowl, sprinkle the gelatin over ¼ cup/2.1 ounces/61 grams of the milk and set aside for 5 minutes to let the gelatin soften.

3. Combine the remaining milk, the sugar, salt, and peanut butter chips in a medium saucepan set over medium-low heat. Cook, stirring constantly, until the chips are melted, about 5 minutes, pressing on the peanut butter chips occasionally to encourage them to melt.

4. When all the chips are melted, remove the pan from the heat and stir in the reserved gelatin mixture until completely smooth and combined. Stir in the peanut butter and vanilla until well combined, then strain the mixture through a fine-mesh sieve into a large bowl. Set aside for 20 minutes to allow the mixture to cool to room temperature, stirring every 5 minutes to discourage premature gelling.

5. In a medium bowl, whip the cream on medium-high speed until stiff peaks form, 1 to 3 minutes. Beating on low speed, slowly drizzle the peanut butter mixture into the whipped cream. Continue beating until the peanut butter mixture is completely incorporated.

INGREDIENT	VOLUME	WEIGHT (STANDARD)	WEIGHT (METRIC)
PB & J CREAM			
Raspberry jam, preferably seedless (see headnote)	¼ cup	2.5 ounces	70 grams
Unflavored powdered gelatin	1½ teaspoons		
Whole milk	¾ cup	6.4 ounces	182 grams
Sugar	¼ cup	1.75 ounces	50 grams
Salt	¼ teaspoon		
Peanut butter baking chips	½ cup	3 ounces	85 grams
Creamy peanut butter	¼ cup	2.4 ounces	68 grams
Vanilla extract	1 teaspoon		
Heavy cream	1 cup	8.2 ounces	232 grams
TOPPING			
Vanilla Whipped Cream (page 257)	½ recipe		
Roasted salted peanuts, chopped	2 tablespoons	0.5 ounce	14 grams

6. FILL THE CRUST: Transfer half the mixture to the cooled pie crust. Pipe a tight spiral of the raspberry jam over the peanut butter cream, starting at the center of the pie and spiraling out toward the outer edge.

7. Carefully scoop dollops of the remaining peanut butter cream on top of the raspberry spiral until it is mostly covered. Smooth the top with an offset spatula, taking care not to disturb the spiral underneath. Refrigerate until the mixture is set, at least 6 hours.

8. MAKE THE TOPPING: Spread the Vanilla Whipped Cream in an even layer over the top of the pie. Sprinkle with the chopped peanuts before serving. (Store any leftovers in the refrigerator for up to 2 days.)

TOFFEE CREAM
with Crunch

WHAT YOU NEED
• Deep-Dish Single Crust (page 36), baked and cooled in a 9½-inch deep-dish pie plate

We were inspired to develop this pie after trying a recipe for homemade Kit-Kat bars. We thought that cracker-y crunch would be a great layer to include in a candy bar–inspired pie. We love how this pie's sweet, velvety brown sugar–cream filling contrasts with the layer of salty, crunchy chocolate-coated "wafers." There is no conceivable universe where this pie is a health food, so feel free to serve slices with Vanilla Whipped Cream (page 257).

1. START THE TOFFEE CREAM: Whisk the milk, 1 cup/8.2 ounces/ 232 grams of the cream, and the cornstarch together in a medium saucepan until the cornstarch has dissolved. Whisk in the brown sugar and salt.

2. Whisk in the eggs one at a time. Over medium heat, bring the mixture to a boil, whisking constantly. Continue whisking the boiling mixture vigorously for 1 minute. The mixture will have thickened.

3. Remove the mixture from the heat. Whisk in the butter, vanilla, and caramel extract until the butter is melted and incorporated. Strain the mixture into a large mixing bowl. Press plastic wrap directly onto the surface of the cream to prevent a skin from forming. Refrigerate the mixture until it's firm and cold throughout, at least 3 hours. (This can be made a day ahead of assembling the pie.)

recipe continues

INGREDIENT	VOLUME	WEIGHT (STANDARD)	WEIGHT (METRIC)
TOFFEE CREAM			
Whole milk	1 cup	8.5 ounces	242 grams
Heavy cream	1⅓ cups	10.9 ounces	309 grams
Cornstarch	¼ cup	1.05 ounces	30 grams
Dark brown sugar, lightly packed	½ cup plus 1 tablespoon	4.05 ounces	115 grams
Salt	¼ teaspoon		
Eggs	2 large		
Unsalted butter	4 tablespoons	2 ounces	57 grams
Vanilla extract	2 teaspoons		
Caramel extract (optional)	½ teaspoon		
CHOCOLATE CRUNCH			
Bittersweet chocolate, finely chopped		8 ounces	227 grams
Heavy cream	½ cup	4.1 ounces	116 grams
Club crackers	about 36	4.4 ounces	126 grams
TOPPING			
Chocolate Ganache (page 264), warm and pourable	¾ recipe		
Toasted sliced almonds	⅓ cup	1 ounce	28 grams

4. MAKE THE CHOCOLATE CRUNCH: In a medium bowl, melt the chocolate together with the cream until combined. This can be done using a microwave at medium (50%) power or over a saucepan of simmering water (see page 27).

5. FILL THE CRUST: Pour ⅓ cup of the chocolate mixture over the bottom of the cooled pie crust. Spread the mixture in an even layer. Press enough crackers into the chocolate to create a single layer of crackers. Break some crackers to fit into the areas near the pie crust edge. Repeat two more times to create 3 layers of chocolate and 3 layers of crackers.

6. Smooth the remaining chocolate over the top of the final cracker layer. Refrigerate while finishing the toffee cream.

7. FINISH THE TOFFEE CREAM: Use an electric mixer to briefly beat the cold toffee cream to break it up, about 10 seconds. Whip the remaining ⅓ cup/2.7 ounces/77 grams of cream until it holds stiff peaks, 1 to 3 minutes. Fold the whipped cream into the toffee cream. Spread the toffee cream over the chocolate-covered crackers. Return the pie to the refrigerator for at least 4 hours to allow the cream to set.

8. MAKE THE TOPPING: Pour the warm Chocolate Ganache over the top of the toffee cream layer and smooth into an even layer. Before the ganache sets, sprinkle the toasted almonds over it. Refrigerate the pie to allow the chocolate to firm up before serving, about 30 minutes. (Store any leftovers in the refrigerator for up to 2 days.)

South Seas
COCONUT DELUXE

Gilded with chocolate, dulce de leche caramel, and toasted coconut, this combo of flavors might remind you of a certain Girl Scout cookie, but really, it's a play on a fancy coconut macaroon cookie in the form of coconut cream pie. The toasted coconut both inside and on top of the pie provides a delicate crunchy contrast to the smooth coconut cream filling.

MAKES ONE 9½-INCH DEEP-DISH PIE

WHAT YOU NEED

- Deep-Dish Single Crust (page 36), baked and cooled in a 9½-inch deep-dish pie plate
- 2 piping bags (see page 21) fitted with Ateco or Wilton #2 round piping tips
- Pie crust shield or foil (see page 19) (optional)

1. MAKE THE BOTTOM LAYER: In a small microwave-safe bowl, gently heat the dulce de leche until it is soft and spreadable with a peanut butter–like consistency, about 1 minute at medium (50%) power. Spread the mixture over the bottom of the cooled pie crust. Refrigerate the pie until the dulce de leche is cold, about 30 minutes.

2. MAKE THE CREAMY COCONUT FILLING: Whisk together the coconut milk, 1 cup/8.2 ounces/232 grams of the cream, and the cornstarch in a medium saucepan until the cornstarch has dissolved. Whisk in the sugar and salt, and then whisk in the eggs one at a time. Turn the heat to medium and bring the mixture to a simmer (a few large bubbles should

recipe continues

INGREDIENT	VOLUME	WEIGHT (STANDARD)	WEIGHT (METRIC)
BOTTOM LAYER			
Dulce de leche	¾ cup	8 ounces	227 grams
CREAMY COCONUT FILLING			
Canned coconut milk (not low-fat)	1 cup	8.25 ounces	234 grams
Heavy cream	1⅓ cups	10.9 ounces	309 grams
Cornstarch	¼ cup	1.05 ounces	30 grams
Sugar	½ cup plus 1 tablespoon	4.05 ounces	115 grams
Salt	¼ teaspoon		
Eggs	2 large		
Unsalted butter, cut into 4 pieces	4 tablespoons	2 ounces	55 grams
Vanilla extract	1 teaspoon		
Sweetened coconut flakes, toasted (see page 28)	⅔ cup	2 ounces	57 grams
CHOCOLATE LAYER			
Chocolate Ganache (page 264), warm and pourable	½ recipe		
TOPPING			
Dulce de leche	2 tablespoons	1.35 ounces	38 grams
Bittersweet chocolate, melted		1.5 ounces	43 grams
Sweetened coconut flakes, toasted (see page 28)	⅓ cup	1 ounce	28 grams

break the surface), whisking constantly. Reduce the heat to medium-low and continue to simmer, whisking constantly, for 1 minute to ensure that the mixture is fully thickened.

3. Remove the saucepan from the heat and whisk in the butter and vanilla until the butter is melted and incorporated. Transfer the mixture to a large mixing bowl. Press plastic wrap directly onto the surface of the cream to prevent a skin from forming and refrigerate until it's firm and cold throughout, at least 3 hours (or up to 1 day), before assembling the pie.

4. ASSEMBLE THE PIE: In a small bowl, using a hand mixer on medium-high speed, whip the remaining ⅓ cup/2.7 ounces/77 grams of cream until it holds stiff peaks, 1 to 3 minutes. Using the same beaters, briefly beat the coconut mixture to break it up, about 10 seconds. Using a rubber spatula, fold the whipped cream and toasted coconut into the coconut cream until the mixture is uniform and no streaks of whipped cream are visible.

5. Spread half of the creamy coconut mixture in a smooth layer over the dulce de leche.

6. ADD THE CHOCOLATE LAYER: Spread the Chocolate Ganache in a smooth layer over the creamy coconut filling while still warm. Spread the remaining coconut filling in a smooth layer over the ganache. Refrigerate the pie until it is cold throughout, about 3 hours (or up to overnight).

7. ADD THE TOPPING: In a small microwave-safe bowl, gently heat the dulce de leche until it is soft and spreadable with a peanut butter–like consistency, 10 to 20 seconds at medium (50%) power. Transfer the warmed dulce de leche to a prepared piping bag and the melted chocolate to the second piping bag.

8. Sprinkle about half the toasted coconut flakes over the top of the pie.

9. To keep the pie crust edge neat, cover with a pie crust shield (if you don't have one, it's okay). Drizzle the warm dulce de leche over the top of the pie. Drizzle the melted chocolate over the top of the pie. You don't have to use all of the dulce de leche or chocolate. Remove the crust shield.

10. While the dulce de leche and chocolate are still warm, sprinkle the remaining toasted coconut around the edge of the pie near the crust. This will help to cover up any chocolate smudges near the crust edge. (Store any leftovers in the refrigerator for up to 2 days. The toasted coconut inside and on top of the pie will be softer on the second day.)

Double Chocolate
MINT CHIP

WHAT YOU NEED
- Cocoa Pastry Crust (page 40), baked and cooled in a 9½-inch deep-dish pie plate
- Piping bag (see page 21) fitted with a Wilton #1M or other large star piping tip

When Chris moved to Atlanta from Pittsburgh, he frequently baked treats to share with his new coworkers (he jokingly considered it job security). A mint chocolate chip layer cake was the all-time favorite, devoured and spoken fondly of like no other, and we learned an important lesson: There is a fandom for mint chocolate chip! This pie is like Chris's cake in pie form. It has a cocoa pastry shell filled with a velvety chocolate ganache layer and is topped with a light mint mousse filled with crunchy chocolate crisped-rice pearls. You can substitute an equal volume of Nestlé Crunch baking pieces or even mini chocolate chips for the chocolate pearls if they prove to be difficult to find.

1. MAKE THE MINT CHIP GANACHE: Place the chopped bittersweet chocolate in a medium heat-safe bowl. Heat the cream in a small saucepan until it begins to simmer (watch it closely so it doesn't boil over), then pour the cream over the chocolate and set aside for 30 seconds. Whisk the hot cream and chopped chocolate together until the mixture is smooth.

2. Transfer the chocolate ganache to the cooled pie crust, smoothing with an offset spatula, if necessary. Sprinkle the chopped chocolate mints over the top of the ganache. Transfer the pie to the refrigerator and chill until the ganache is set, about 2 hours.

3. MAKE THE MINT CHOCOLATE CHIP CREAM: Sprinkle the gelatin over 2 tablespoons water in a small microwave-safe bowl and set aside. In a medium saucepan, whisk together the egg yolks, sugar, and milk. Whisking constantly, cook the mixture over medium-low heat until it is slightly thickened and reaches 160°F on an instant-read thermometer,

recipe continues

INGREDIENT	VOLUME	WEIGHT (STANDARD)	WEIGHT (METRIC)
MINT CHIP GANACHE			
Bittersweet chocolate, chopped		8 ounces	227 grams
Heavy cream	1 cup plus 2 tablespoons	9.2 ounces	261 grams
Chocolate mints, such as Andes, chopped	½ cup (about 17 mints)	2.8 ounces	80 grams
MINT CHOCOLATE CHIP CREAM			
Unflavored powdered gelatin	2½ teaspoons		
Egg yolks	3 large		
Sugar	½ cup	3.5 ounces	100 grams
Whole milk	½ cup	4.25 ounces	120 grams
White chocolate, melted		8 ounces	227 grams
Green crème de menthe	2 tablespoons	1 ounce	28 grams
Mint green gel food color (optional)	1 to 2 drops		
Heavy cream	1½ cups	12.3 ounces	348 grams
Chocolate pearls, preferably Valrhona (see headnote)	⅓ cup	1.6 ounces	45 grams
TOPPING			
Cocoa Whipped Cream (page 258)	1 recipe		

about 5 minutes. The mixture will coat the back of a spoon when it is properly thickened. Remove the egg mixture from the heat and continue whisking it to cool it slightly, 1 to 2 minutes.

4. Heat the gelatin mixture in the microwave on high (100%) power in 5-second intervals, checking and stirring it until it just begins to bubble at the edges and the gelatin is dissolved (don't let it boil). Whisk the gelatin into the egg mixture.

5. Whisk the melted white chocolate into the egg mixture until smooth. Strain the mixture through a fine-mesh sieve into a medium bowl. Whisk in the crème de menthe and mint green color, if using. Allow the mixture to cool to room temperature, 15 to 20 minutes, stirring occasionally to prevent premature gelling.

6. In a large bowl (or using a stand mixer fitted with the whisk attachment), whip the cream on medium-high speed until it holds stiff peaks, 1 to 3 minutes. Reduce the speed to low and slowly drizzle in the mint–white chocolate mixture until it is completely incorporated. Fold in the chocolate pearls.

7. Transfer the mint chocolate chip cream to the chilled pie, smoothing with an offset spatula. Return the pie to the refrigerator and allow it to chill until the mint cream layer is set, 4 to 6 hours (or up to overnight).

8. MAKE THE TOPPING: Transfer the Cocoa Whipped Cream to the piping bag. Pipe a ring of the cocoa whipped cream around the edge of the pie before serving. (Store any leftovers in the refrigerator for up to 2 days.)

Variation:
HOLIDAY PINK MINT CHIP

Follow the instructions for the Double Chocolate Mint Chip pie, substituting white crème de menthe for the green and pink or red food color for the mint green gel food color. The result is a pink and brown mint pie that is wintertime dessert-table friendly and makes a great Valentine's Day pie!

BLUE RIBBON BONUS: *The Drizzled Crust*

Drizzling a pie crust with colored melted candy coating (see page 27) adds a fun, Jackson Pollock-like look to your pie. For the Double Chocolate Mint Chip pie on page 63, you will need 30 discs (1.75 ounces/50 grams) of white candy coating and 10 discs (0.6 ounces/17 grams) of any color candy coating (we like green). Melt 20 of the white candy coating discs in a small microwave-safe bowl at medium (50%) power, stirring every 20 seconds, until the discs are melted and smooth. Transfer to a piping bag fitted with a #2 piping tip. Repeat with the remaining 10 white and the tinted candy coating discs, melting them together to create a pastel shade. Transfer that to a second piping bag fitted with a #2 piping tip. Carefully remove the cooled chocolate crust from the pan to a double layer of paper towels on a baking sheet. If the crust does not seem like it's going to come out in one piece, abort the mission and drizzle the candy coating over the crust still in the pan (removing it from the pan keeps the candy coating from mucking up the outside of the pie pan, so drizzle carefully).

Drizzle the coating over the edge of the crust, allowing the excess coating to land on the outside of the crust. Some chocolate will land in the crust, but that is fine because it will be covered with the filling. You will not use all of the melted candy coating, but it is difficult to melt effectively using smaller amounts. Allow the coating to set for about 10 minutes before returning the crust to the pan and filling the pie. You can do this technique on any blind-baked pie crust using about 20 candy melts of any color. Use pink candy coating for the Holiday Pink Mint Chip pie variation.

The Chocolate
CHOCOLATE CHIP

MAKES ONE 9½-INCH DEEP-DISH PIE

WHAT YOU NEED

- Pie dough for Standard Single Crust (page 35), still in a disc shape and not rolled
- Graham Cracker Crust (page 48), baked and cooled in a 9½-inch deep-dish plate with no lip
- Extra butter or cooking spray for greasing the pan

This pie is a tribute to another classic American dessert: the chocolate chip cookie. We use browned butter (butter cooked until the milk solids turn brown) to make the cookie dough for this pie. Don't worry: we toast the flour and don't use any eggs, making this cookie dough completely safe to eat! The nuggets of cookie dough are added to decadent chocolate mousse and topped with a giant chocolate chip pie crust cookie.

1. MAKE THE COOKIE DOUGH: Line a 9 by 5-inch loaf pan with parchment and lightly grease the parchment with cooking spray or softened butter. Add the flour to a medium saucepan and toast it over medium heat, stirring constantly, until the flour has a light beige color and nutty aroma (if it gets too dark, start over—no one likes bitter cookie dough). Transfer the flour to a small bowl to cool completely.

2. Carefully wipe the saucepan with a damp towel (you can let it cool first if you want). In the same saucepan, melt 4 tablespoons/2 ounces/ 57 grams of the butter over medium heat. Continue cooking until the butter is golden brown and has a nutty aroma, about 2 minutes.

recipe continues

INGREDIENT	VOLUME	WEIGHT (STANDARD)	WEIGHT (METRIC)
COOKIE DOUGH			
All-purpose flour	½ cup plus 2 tablespoons	3.15 ounces	89 grams
Unsalted butter	5 tablespoons	2.5 ounces	71 grams
Granulated sugar	3 tablespoons	1.3 ounces	38 grams
Light brown sugar, lightly packed	3 tablespoons	1.3 ounces	38 grams
Heavy cream	1 tablespoon	0.5 ounce	15 grams
Vanilla extract	½ teaspoon		
Salt	¼ teaspoon		
Chocolate pearls or substitute mini semisweet chocolate chips	¼ cup	1.2 ounces	34 grams
PIE DOUGH COOKIE TOP CRUST			
Whole milk	1 tablespoon		
Semisweet chocolate chips	¼ cup	1.5 ounces	43 grams
CHOCOLATE MOUSSE			
Heavy cream, cold	1 cup	8.2 ounces	232 grams
Egg	1 large		
Granulated sugar	⅓ cup	2.35 ounces	67 grams
Salt	pinch		
Bittersweet chocolate, melted and still warm		6 ounces	170 grams
TOPPING			
Chocolate Ganache (page 264), warm and pourable	¾ recipe		

Transfer the browned butter to a large bowl and stir in the remaining 1 tablespoon/0.5 ounce/14 grams of butter until it's completely melted. Set aside until the butter is room temperature and begins to firm up around the edge, about 30 minutes, depending on the temperature of your kitchen.

3. Whisk the granulated and brown sugars into the melted butter. Whisk in the cream, vanilla, and salt. Fold in the toasted flour until the mixture forms a batter, then fold in the chocolate pearls.

4. Spread the batter in the prepared loaf pan, cover the pan with plastic wrap, and refrigerate until the mixture is cold and firm, about 2 hours or overnight. After the dough is firm, transfer the block of dough to a cutting board. Use a sharp knife to cut the dough into ½-inch cubes. Return the dough cubes to the refrigerator until you assemble the pie.

5. MAKE THE PIE DOUGH COOKIE TOP CRUST: Roll out the pie dough to a ⅛-inch thickness. Cut out an 8- to 9-inch circle in the dough using a pan lid or cake pan as a guide (pie scraps can be kept and frozen for another time). Transfer the dough circle to a sheet of parchment or a silicone baking mat set on a baking sheet. Brush the top of the dough round with the milk, then sprinkle the chocolate chips over the circle and lightly press them into the dough so they are adhered and won't roll around. Freeze the chocolate chip pie dough disc for at least 20 minutes or up to overnight. Preheat the oven to 350°F.

6. Bake the crust until the top and bottom of the round are both golden brown, about 30 minutes. Transfer the pie dough cookie to a cooling rack to cool completely, about 30 minutes.

7. MAKE THE CHOCOLATE MOUSSE: Using a stand mixer or hand mixer, whip the cream in a medium bowl at medium-high speed until it holds stiff peaks, 1 to 3 minutes, and return it to the refrigerator.

8. Bring a medium saucepan filled with 1 inch of water to a simmer. In a large heat-safe bowl, whisk the egg, sugar, and salt together and place the bowl over the simmering water (make sure the bottom of the bowl doesn't touch the water). Reduce the heat to low, and constantly whisk until the sugar is dissolved and the mixture is 160°F using an instant-read thermometer. Remove the bowl from over the water and, using a hand mixer or whisk (there is not enough volume to effectively use a stand mixer), continue beating the mixture until it is thick and begins to hold a slight trail in the wake of the beaters (or whisk), 2 to 3 minutes. Whisk in the warm melted chocolate (it's okay if the mixture looks stiff and grainy). Whisk in about a third of the whipped cream, and once the mixture is lightened, gently fold in the remaining whipped cream until the chocolate mousse is uniform without any white streaks.

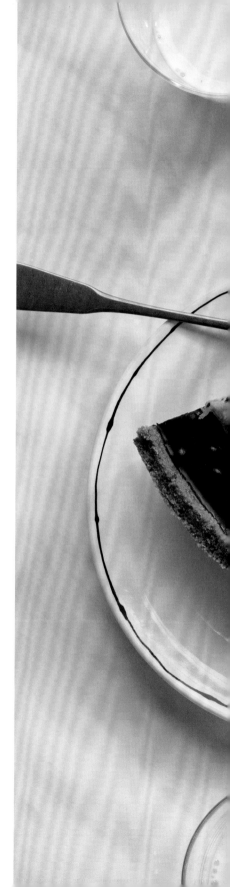

9. Fold the chilled cookie dough cubes into the chocolate mousse. Smooth the mousse into the cooled crumb crust. Refrigerate the pie until the mousse is cold and set, 1 to 2 hours.

10. **ADD THE TOPPING:** When the mousse is cold and set, pour the Chocolate Ganache over the top of the chocolate mousse layer and smooth into an even layer. Immediately press the pie dough cookie top crust into the ganache. Return to the refrigerator to fully chill before serving, about 3 to 4 hours. (Store any leftovers in the refrigerator for up to 2 days.)

The 6151 RICHMOND

WHAT YOU NEED

- Nut Graham Cracker Crust (page 50) made using pecans, baked and cooled in a 9½-inch deep-dish pie plate with no lip

Chris's all-time favorite show is *The Golden Girls*, and this cheesecake pie—they were always gathering around a cheesecake, after all!—is a tribute to their sass, wisdom, and hilarity. The flavors each represent one of the show's four characters: a pecan crust for Georgia-born southern belle Blanche Devereaux; Italian limoncello liqueur for the mom-and-daughter duo Sophia Petrillo and Dorothy Zbornak; and Scandinavian lingonberry jam to represent St. Olaf Woman of the Year Rose Nylund. Sweet-tart lingonberries taste similar to cranberries; they are most often found as a jam or preserve (see Sources, page 265). If you can't find lingonberry jam or preserves, you can substitute another berry, like raspberry or strawberry.

1. Add the limoncello to a small microwave-safe bowl. Sprinkle the gelatin over the top and set aside.

2. In a large bowl, beat the cream cheese until smooth and creamy using a hand mixer on medium speed (or using a stand mixer fitted with the paddle attachment). Reduce the speed to low and beat in the confectioners' sugar, salt, and vanilla; increase the speed to medium and beat until just combined.

3. Microwave the gelatin mixture for 20 to 30 seconds, stirring every 5 seconds, until the gelatin has dissolved and the mixture is just bubbling at the edges. Beat the warm gelatin into the cream cheese mixture.

4. While mixing, slowly pour in the cream and continue beating on medium speed until the mixture is light and fluffy, 1 to 2 minutes. Pour the filling into the prepared crust and smooth the top. Dollop the jam over the top of the filling. Using the back of a spoon or an offset spatula, create swoops and swirls on the top of the pie, incompletely incorporating the jam into the swirls in a design of your choosing. Refrigerate the pie for at least 6 hours before serving. (Store any leftovers in the refrigerator for up 3 days. Wrapped tightly in foil and placed in a large zippered plastic bag, this pie can be frozen for up to 1 month.)

INGREDIENT	VOLUME	WEIGHT (STANDARD)	WEIGHT (METRIC)
Lemon liqueur, preferably limoncello	¼ cup	2.1 ounces	60 grams
Unflavored powdered gelatin	2½ teaspoons		
Cream cheese, at room temperature	3 8-ounce packages	24 ounces	680 grams
Confectioners' sugar	1¼ cups	5 ounces	142 grams
Salt	pinch		
Vanilla extract	1 teaspoon		
Heavy cream	1¼ cups	10.25 ounces	290 grams
Lingonberry jam or preserves (see headnote)	⅔ cup	6.5 ounces	184 grams

MOCHA
Mystery

The mystery in this pie is the addition of chipotle powder, a spice made from ground smoked chipotle chiles. The chipotle powder pairs beautifully with chocolate and adds a slight, warm glow of heat. It's not enough to say that the pie is "hot," but the hint of smokiness combined with the chopped chocolate-covered espresso beans will make your guests wonder what the mystery ingredient is in this mocha pie. If you want to take the pie to the next level, see the Blue Ribbon Bonus, opposite, on how to make confectionery lace.

MAKES ONE 9-INCH PIE
WHAT YOU NEED
• Cocoa Pastry Crust (page 40), baked and cooled in a standard 9-inch pie plate

1. MAKE THE MOCHA CHEESECAKE FILLING: Beat together the cream cheese and confectioners' sugar with an electric mixer until smooth. Beat in the sour cream, coffee liqueur, vanilla, salt, espresso powder, chipotle powder, and melted chocolate until the mixture is creamy and uniform.

2. Spread about 2 cups (11.5 ounces/325 grams) of the cheesecake mixture into the prepared pie crust. Sprinkle the chopped espresso beans over the filling and gently press them into the cheesecake layer to keep them in place. Smooth the remaining cheesecake mixture over the espresso beans. Refrigerate until cold, at least 1 hour and up to overnight.

3. MAKE THE TOPPING: Spread the Chocolate Ganache over the top of the pie while still warm and pourable. Refrigerate until the ganache has set, about 2 hours before serving. (Store any leftovers in the refrigerator for up to 3 days. The chocolate-covered espresso beans will be less crunchy on the second day.)

INGREDIENT	VOLUME	WEIGHT (STANDARD)	WEIGHT (METRIC)
MOCHA CHEESECAKE FILLING			
Cream cheese, at room temperature	2¼ 8-ounce packages	18 ounces	510 grams
Confectioners' sugar	¾ cup	3 ounces	85 grams
Sour cream, at room temperature	3 tablespoons	1.6 ounces	45 grams
Coffee liqueur, such as Kahlúa	2 tablespoons	1.2 ounces	34 grams
Vanilla extract	1 teaspoon		
Salt	pinch		
Instant espresso powder	2 teaspoons		
Chipotle powder	⅜ teaspoon		
Semisweet chocolate, melted		6 ounces	170 grams
Chocolate-covered espresso beans, chopped	½ cup	3 ounces	85 grams
TOPPING			
Chocolate Ganache (page 264), warm and pourable	¾ recipe		

Confectionery Lace

The addition of white edible lace (see page 13) adds a beautiful contrast to the dark chocolate glaze and crust. To make the edible lace, prepare confectionery lace mix (page 13) according to the manufacturer's instructions. Spread the prepared confectionery lace mix onto a silicone lace mat (page 22) with a design at least 8½ inches square. Allow the mix to set according to the manufacturer's instructions. When set, remove the decoration from the mat and use a clean pair of scissors to cut the lace to an 8½-inch circle. Keep the lace round covered in a sealed zippered storage bag to prevent it from drying out while preparing the pie. Place the lace round on top of the chocolate ganache topping immediately (but carefully!) after spreading it over the top of the pie.

Hot Fudge à l'Orange
BROWNIE SUNDAE

This sundae-inspired vanilla cream pie elevates the hot fudge brownie sundae with hints of orange and chunks of from-scratch brownies. With its cold creaminess, each slice of pie begs to be doused with a warm batch of thick homemade fudge sauce.

MAKES ONE 9½-INCH DEEP-DISH PIE

WHAT YOU NEED

- Cocoa Graham Cracker Crust (page 50), baked and cooled in a 9½-inch deep-dish pan with no lip
- Extra butter or cooking spray for greasing the pan
- 1 recipe Hot Fudge Sauce (page 260), for serving
- ¾ recipe Vanilla Whipped Cream (optional; page 257), for serving

1. MAKE THE ORANGE BROWNIES: Preheat the oven to 350°F. Line the bottom and sides of an 8½ by 4½-inch loaf pan with aluminum foil or parchment. Grease the foil with butter or cooking spray and set aside.

2. In a large bowl, whisk together the melted bittersweet chocolate, butter, and cocoa powder. Whisk in the orange zest, egg, vanilla, and Cointreau. Whisk in the brown sugar until the mixture is uniform, then whisk in the

recipe continues

INGREDIENT	VOLUME	WEIGHT (STANDARD)	WEIGHT (METRIC)
ORANGE BROWNIES (bake up to 2 days before serving)			
Bittersweet chocolate, melted		1 ounce	28 grams
Unsalted butter, melted	4 tablespoons	2 ounces	57 grams
Dutch-process cocoa powder	4 teaspoons	0.25 ounce	7 grams
Finely grated orange zest	1 teaspoon		
Egg, at room temperature	1 large		
Vanilla extract	1 teaspoon		
Cointreau orange liqueur	1 teaspoon		
Light brown sugar, lightly packed	⅔ cup	4.65 ounces	133 grams
Water, boiling	¼ cup	2.1 ounces	59 grams
All-purpose flour	½ cup	2.5 ounces	71 grams
Salt	⅛ teaspoon		
VANILLA-ORANGE CREAM			
Granulated sugar	½ cup plus 1 tablespoon	4.05 ounces	115 grams
Finely grated orange zest	1 teaspoon		
Whole milk	1 cup	8.5 ounces	242 grams
Heavy cream, cold	1⅓ cups	10.9 ounces	309 grams
Cornstarch	¼ cup	1.05 ounces	30 grams
Salt	¼ teaspoon		
Eggs	2 large		
Unsalted butter	4 tablespoons	2 ounces	57 grams
Vanilla bean paste	2 teaspoons		
Cointreau orange liqueur (optional)	1 teaspoon		

boiling water. Fold in the flour and salt until no white streaks of flour are visible.

3. Pour the brownie batter into the prepared loaf pan. Bake until a toothpick inserted into the center comes out with just a few moist crumbs, about 15 minutes. Cool the brownies completely in the pan, about 2 hours.

4. Once cooled, lift the brownies from the pan using the foil and transfer the brownies to a cutting board. Cut the brownie block into roughly ½-inch cubes. Place one half in an airtight container and then in the refrigerator. Place the second half of the cubes into a second container and freeze for 1 hour. When the brownie cubes are frozen, use a food processor to grind the brownie cubes into a coarse brownie crumble, 10 to 20 pulses. Transfer the processed brownie to an airtight container in the refrigerator.

5. MAKE THE VANILLA-ORANGE CREAM: In a medium saucepan, rub the granulated sugar and orange zest between your thumbs and fingertips until the sugar is fragrant and uniformly orange. Whisk the milk, 1 cup/ 8.2 ounces/232 grams of the cream, the cornstarch, and salt together until the cornstarch has dissolved. Whisk in the eggs one at a time.

6. Over medium heat, bring the mixture to a simmer (a few large bubbles should break the surface), whisking constantly. Reduce the heat to medium-low and continue to simmer, whisking constantly, for 1 minute to ensure that the mixture is fully thickened.

7. Remove the saucepan from the heat and whisk in the butter, vanilla bean paste, and Cointreau, if using, until the butter is melted and incorporated. Transfer the mixture to a large mixing bowl. Press plastic wrap directly onto the surface of the cream to prevent a skin from forming and refrigerate until it's firm and cold throughout, at least 3 hours (or up to 1 day), before assembling the pie.

8. In a medium bowl, whip the remaining ⅓ cup/2.7 ounces/77 grams cream until it holds stiff peaks, 1 to 3 minutes. Remove the vanilla-orange cream from the refrigerator, discard the plastic, and use an electric mixer to briefly beat the cold cream to break it up, about 10 seconds. Fold the whipped cream into the vanilla-orange cream. Spread about 1 cup of the cream into the cooled pie crust. Sprinkle the brownie cubes evenly over the top of the cream. Spread the remaining cream over the brownie cubes.

9. Smooth the top of the vanilla-orange cream with an offset spatula. Sprinkle the brownie crumbs evenly over the entire top, all the way to the crust edge. Refrigerate the pie for at least 4 hours. Serve with Hot Fudge Sauce and a dollop of Vanilla Whipped Cream, if using. (Store any leftovers in the refrigerator.)

THAI ICED TEA

with Whipped Cream
"Ice Cubes"

Thai iced tea is one of the must-have treats when we have lunch at one of the many Thai restaurants in Atlanta. The mixture of aromatic Thai tea topped with a float of sweetened condensed milk served over ice is a decadent delight we can't go without. This creamy pie's flavor is a spot-on match to the drink, and the whipped cream "ice cubes" complete the look. If you can't find Thai tea mix (see page 265), order a Thai tea with no ice and no condensed milk to go from your local Thai restaurant (you'll need 1½ cups) and use it instead.

MAKES ONE 9-INCH PIE

WHAT YOU NEED
• Standard Single Crust (page 35), baked and cooled in a standard 9-inch pie plate
• Extra butter or cooking spray for greasing the pan

1. MAKE THE THAI TEA CREAM: Brew the Thai tea by steeping the Thai tea mix in the boiling water for 6 minutes. Strain the tea using a fine-mesh sieve. Measure out 1½ cups of tea and set aside to cool.

2. In a medium saucepan, whisk together the cooled tea, whole milk, and cornstarch until the cornstarch is dissolved and then whisk in the sugar, condensed milk, egg yolks, and salt. Over medium heat, bring the mixture to a simmer (a few large bubbles should break the surface), whisking constantly. Reduce the heat to medium-low and continue to simmer, whisking constantly, for 1 minute to ensure that the mixture is fully thickened.

recipe continues

INGREDIENT	VOLUME	WEIGHT (STANDARD)	WEIGHT (METRIC)
THAI TEA CREAM			
Thai tea mix, such as Pantai Norasingh (see headnote)	⅓ cup	1 ounce	28 grams
Water, boiling	2 cups	16.7 ounces	472 grams
Whole milk	½ cup	4.25 ounces	121 grams
Cornstarch	¼ cup	1.05 ounces	30 grams
Sugar	2 tablespoons	0.9 ounce	25 grams
Sweetened condensed milk	1 14-ounce can	14 ounces	397 grams
Egg yolks	4 large		
Salt	pinch		
Unsalted butter	3 tablespoons	1.5 ounces	43 grams
Vanilla extract	2 teaspoons		
VANILLA WHIPPED CREAM "ICE CUBES"			
Vanilla Whipped Cream (page 257), stabilized (so the cubes hold their shape)	½ recipe		
DECORATION			
Brightly colored pesticide-free petals from edible flowers such as nasturtium, echinacea, or violets, for decoration (optional)			

3. Remove the pan from the heat and whisk in the butter and vanilla until the butter has melted and is incorporated. Strain the mixture through a fine-mesh sieve and then pour the tea cream into the cooled pie crust and smooth the top. Press plastic wrap onto the top of the cream and refrigerate until cold throughout, at least 4 hours or up to overnight.

4. MAKE THE VANILLA WHIPPED CREAM "ICE CUBES": Grease the bottom and sides of a 9 by 5-inch loaf pan with butter or cooking spray. Line the long side of the pan with a 14 by 8-inch strip of parchment (or waxed paper) and grease the parchment.

5. Evenly spread the whipped cream into the prepared loaf pan. Freeze the mixture until completely frozen, at least 4 hours or up to 8 hours. It is important that the mixture is completely frozen before continuing. Remove the frozen whipped cream from the freezer, run a thin knife along the edges of the cream to loosen it from the pan, and lift the parchment sling out of the pan. Turn it out onto a cutting board. Using a sharp knife, cut the frozen whipped cream into 1-inch squares to create cubes. Remove the plastic wrap from the pie. Arrange the cubes over the top of the pie.

6. Refrigerate the pie for at least 2 hours or up to overnight before serving to allow the frozen whipped cream cubes to thaw (they will keep their shape because of the piping gel). For an additional pop of color, garnish with the edible flower petals before serving, if desired. (Store any leftovers in the refrigerator—but that said, the pie is best eaten within 2 days of making the Thai Tea Cream.)

PIE *of the* TIGER

MAKES ONE 9½-INCH DEEP-DISH PIE

WHAT YOU NEED

- Cocoa Graham Cracker Crust (page 50), baked and cooled in a 9½-inch deep-dish pie plate (the deepest you have) up to 1 day ahead
- Tiger stripe stencil (we use a zebra stripe stencil, and unless you're a zoologist, you probably won't notice)
- Piping bag (see page 21) fitted with a Wilton #66 or other small leaf or star piping tip

Nabisco Famous Chocolate Wafers have been used for decades to create the simplest "cake" ever: stacks of cookies layered and smothered with whipped cream that soften in the refrigerator, transforming into a chocolate cream layer "cake." This pie is the next step in the evolution of the famous wafer. We arrange the cookies in a cocoa-infused mascarpone cream, creating a cute tiger-striped slice of pie with a cocoa-stenciled tiger stripe on top.

1. MAKE THE FILLING: Place the cream in a microwave-safe bowl and microwave on high until just starting to boil. Sift the cocoa and espresso powder into the heated cream and stir with a whisk until dissolved. Add the sugar and continue whisking until the sugar is dissolved. Cover the bowl with plastic wrap and place in the refrigerator until completely cold, at least 2 hours or up to 1 day before completing the filling.

2. Add the mascarpone cheese to the cold cream and beat with a hand mixer until the mixture has thickened and holds stiff peaks, 3 to 5 minutes. Spread the filling in the cooled crust.

3. Break the first few wafers into shards approximately ¾ by 2 inches in size. Feel free to make use of any already broken cookies in the box for this purpose. Insert a small wafer shard upright into the center of the pie. Continue inserting shards of wafers into the pie so that their edges are almost touching, forming a continuous line that spirals to the outer edge of the pie. There should be approximately ½ inch of filling between each row of wafers. The shards of can get larger in size in the outer rows of the spiral.

4. After inserting all of the wafer shards, you'll notice that the filling may have risen unevenly. Use an offset spatula to smooth the filling back down as much as possible. It is okay if the tips of the wafers are still poking through a bit. They are about to be covered by the topping.

INGREDIENT	VOLUME	WEIGHT (STANDARD)	WEIGHT (METRIC)
FILLING			
Heavy cream	1½ cups	12.3 ounces	348 grams
Dutch-process cocoa powder	6 tablespoons	1.15 ounces	32 grams
Instant espresso powder	1 teaspoon		
Sugar	1⅓ cups	9.35 ounces	265 grams
Mascarpone cheese	2 cups	16 ounces	454 grams
Nabisco Famous Chocolate Wafers	about 35 cookies	about 7 ounces	about 200 grams
TOPPING			
Vanilla Whipped Cream (page 257), stabilized	1 recipe		
Dutch-process cocoa powder	2 tablespoons	0.4 ounce	11 grams

MAKE THE TOPPING: Spread all the stabilized Vanilla Whipped Cream across the surface of the pie, mounding any extra topping toward the middle. Place a metal pie crust shield on top of the pie. The opening should be touching the cream. Using a long straight metal spatula, scrape along the surface of the pie crust shield, removing the excess cream and creating a beautifully smooth surface. Transfer this scraped off cream into the prepared piping bag.

6. Place a tiger stripe stencil on top of the cream and sift the cocoa powder onto the surface of the pie. Carefully remove the stencil to avoid spilling cocoa on the pie or making a mess in your kitchen. Remove the pie crust shield. Pipe a small border along the edge of the crust to cover any stray marks left by the pie crust shield.

7. Place the pie in the refrigerator for at least 6 hours or preferably overnight. This will allow the wafers to soften into vertical cakey stripes. (Store any leftovers in the refrigerator for up to 3 days.)

PITTSBURGH PROUD

MAKES ONE 9½-INCH DEEP-DISH PIE

WHAT YOU NEED

- Cocoa Pastry Crust (page 40), preferably made with black cocoa, baked and cooled in a 9½-inch deep-dish pie plate
- Soft food-safe paintbrush (optional)

Chris spent ten years in college and graduate school in Pittsburgh, and he still misses it sometimes (until he sees a winter weather report). One of the many great things about the Steel City is ordering something "Pittsburgh-style," meaning it's topped with french fries—be it a burger or your salad. This creamy Pittsburgh-style chocolate pie is crowned with salty, chocolate-covered potato sticks (our confectionery ode to the french fry) and adorned with flakes of edible gold. For an authentic treat, make this black-and-gold pie with Dark Brewed Porter from Pittsburgh-based Yuengling brewing company.

1. MAKE THE CHOCOLATE MALT CREAM: In a 4-cup glass measuring cup, microwave the porter on high (100%) power until the mixture is reduced to ¼ cup, 6 to 10 minutes. Alternatively, bring the beer to a boil in a medium saucepan over medium heat and continue to boil, stirring occasionally, until it is reduced to ¼ cup.

2. In the bowl of a stand mixer, whisk together 2 tablespoons of the reduced porter, the brown sugar, malted milk powder, salt, and eggs. Place the bowl over a saucepan of simmering water and heat the mixture until it reaches 160°F on an instant-read thermometer, whisking constantly.

3. Transfer the bowl to a stand mixer fitted with a whisk attachment. Beat the mixture on medium-high speed until it has thickened and cooled and the outside of the bowl no longer feels warm, 6 to 8 minutes.

recipe continues

INGREDIENT	VOLUME	WEIGHT (STANDARD)	WEIGHT (METRIC)
CHOCOLATE MALT CREAM			
Porter beer (see headnote)	¾ cup	6.35 ounces	180 grams
Light brown sugar, lightly packed	1 cup	7 ounces	200 grams
Malted milk powder	3 tablespoons	0.75 ounce	21 grams
Salt	⅛ teaspoon		
Eggs	4 large		
Unsweetened chocolate, melted		4 ounces	113 grams
Semisweet chocolate, melted		4 ounces	113 grams
Unsalted butter, cut into 4 chunks, at room temperature	8 tablespoons	4 ounces	113 grams
Vanilla extract	½ teaspoon		
Heavy cream	1 cup plus 2 tablespoons	9.2 ounces	261 grams
CHOCOLATE-COVERED "FRIES"			
Potato sticks (we use Pik-Nik Original Shoestring Potatoes, but use what's available)	2 cups	3 ounces	84 grams
Semisweet chocolate, melted		4 ounces	113 grams
Edible gold leaf, for decoration (optional; see Sources, page 265)			

4. On medium speed, beat in the melted unsweetened and semisweet chocolates, followed by the softened butter, vanilla, and the remaining 2 tablespoons of the reduced porter until just combined.

5. **FILL THE CRUST:** In a separate bowl, and using a whisk or hand mixer (or a separate bowl for your stand mixer), whip the cream on medium-high speed until it holds stiff peaks, 1 to 3 minutes. Gently fold the whipped cream into the chocolate mixture, being sure to scrape the sides and bottom of the bowl until no white streaks remain. Smooth the mixture into the pie crust. Refrigerate the pie for at least 4 hours or up to overnight.

6. **MAKE THE CHOCOLATE-COVERED "FRIES":** In a large bowl, toss together the potato sticks and melted chocolate until the sticks are completely coated. (Any uncoated potato sticks will soften and become mushy in the refrigerator.)

7. Delicately arrange the coated potato sticks across the top of the pie, stacking the sticks high and mighty (a thin layer means that the sticks are packed too tightly) and trying to ensure no clumps are too dense (dense clumps of potato sticks will be difficult to cut through and serve). If decorating with the gold leaf, use a soft food-safe paintbrush to adhere small flakes of the gold to the chocolate-coated potato sticks before the chocolate sets. Refrigerate for at least 30 minutes before serving. (Store any leftovers in the refrigerator. The pie is best eaten within 2 days.)

Variation:
You can make this pie using the Cocoa Graham Cracker Crust (page 50).

Tip: **TRANSPORTING PIES**

With just the two of us at home (our cats don't much care for pie), a lot of our pie creations are transported to either the office or someone else's house to be enjoyed. For transporting whole pies, we find that cake carriers are the best solution. Cake carriers are tall plastic domes designed for safely transporting layer cakes. The high plastic lid ensures that even the highest pile of meringue or whipped cream won't be smooshed. These carriers can be found online or at some kitchen supply stores. We've also had great success with less-expensive cake carriers available at the local dollar store. In a pinch, we have even seen people transporting pies in a large lidded Dutch oven or a photocopy paper box. We also suggest using pieces of nonslip shelf liner from the supermarket or dollar store to help prevent the pie plate from sliding around during sudden starts and stops while on the move. Whatever container you use, make sure to think about how you will transport your pie before you turn on your oven. These pies are too good to wind up upside down on the floor of your car!

Fizzy ROOT BEER FLOAT

MAKES ONE 9½-INCH DEEP-DISH PIE

WHAT YOU NEED

- Deep-Dish Single Crust (page 36), baked and cooled in a 9½-inch deep-dish pie plate
- Piping bag (see page 21) fitted with a Wilton #1M or other large star piping tip, or a 2-tablespoon ice cream or cookie scoop

Chris's first version of this pie earned him his first blue ribbon at the National Pie Championships in the Innovation category. The cool, creamy root beer filling topped with smooth layers of root beer whipped cream tastes *exactly* like a root beer float, while the POP ROCKS (see Sources, page 265) provide a surprising fizz that truly completes the experience. Each slice is topped with a rolled edible "straw" and a cherry on top.

1. MAKE THE ROOT BEER CREAM: In a small bowl, sprinkle the gelatin over 2 tablespoons/1.05 ounces/30 grams of the milk and set aside. Combine the remaining 6 tablespoons/3.2 ounces/91 grams of the milk, the sugar, salt, and white chocolate chips in a medium saucepan. Cook over medium-low heat, stirring constantly, until the chips are melted, about 5 minutes, pressing on the chocolate chips to encourage them to melt.

2. Remove the pan from the heat and stir in the gelatin mixture until it is completely melted. Stir in the root beer soda syrup and root beer concentrate. Strain the mixture into a large bowl using a fine-mesh sieve. Set aside for 20 minutes to allow the mixture to cool to room temperature, stirring every 5 minutes to discourage premature gelling.

recipe continues

INGREDIENT	VOLUME	WEIGHT (STANDARD)	WEIGHT (METRIC)
ROOT BEER CREAM			
Unflavored powdered gelatin	1½ teaspoons		
Whole milk	½ cup	4.25 ounces	121 grams
Sugar	¼ cup	1.75 ounces	50 grams
Salt	¼ teaspoon		
White chocolate chips	½ cup	3 ounces	85 grams
Root beer soda syrup, preferably SodaStream brand (see page 265)	½ cup	5.6 ounces	160 grams
Root beer concentrate, preferably McCormick brand (see page 265)	1 teaspoon		
Heavy cream	1 cup	8.2 ounces	232 grams
Chocolate POP ROCKS, or Pie-Proof Popping Sugar (page 265)	5 0.33-ounce packets	1.65 ounces	47 grams
TOPPING			
Vanilla Bean Whipped Cream (page 258)	1 recipe		
Root Beer Whipped Cream (page 258)	1 recipe		
Maraschino cherries, drained and blotted dry	12 cherries		
Vanilla rolled wafer cookies, such as Pepperidge Farm Pirouette, cut in half cross-wise	12 cookies		

3. In a medium bowl, whip the cream on medium-high speed until it holds stiff peaks, 1 to 3 minutes. Beating on low speed, slowly drizzle the root beer mixture into the whipped cream. Continue beating until it is completely incorporated. Transfer the mixture to the cooled pie crust.

4. After the pie has chilled for 1 hour, sprinkle the POP ROCKS evenly over the top of the pie and gently press them into the cream. Refrigerate until set, at least 3 hours or up to overnight.

5. **MAKE THE TOPPING:** Smooth the Vanilla Bean Whipped Cream over the POP ROCKS to create an even layer. Use the piping bag or an ice cream scoop to portion 12 mounds of the Root Beer Whipped Cream evenly around the pie (one mound for each slice).

6. Top each mound of Root Beer Whipped Cream with a cherry. Insert a rolled wafer cookie into each slice just before serving to keep them crisp. (Store any leftovers in the refrigerator for up to 2 days.)

MASTERING THE WEDGE:
Cutting the Perfect Pie Slice

The best tool for cutting a slice of pie is a thin, sharp knife. Insert the tip of the knife into the center of the pie and draw the knife slowly back to the crust's edge, making sure that the tip of the knife is cutting through the bottom of the crust. When you reach the side crust, continue cutting through the crust with the knife. To cut the crimped pie crust edge, lower the blade of the knife and use a gentle back-and-forth sawing motion. Clean off the blade and reinsert it into the center of the pie to make the second cut of the first slice of pie, following the same technique. Before removing that first slice of pie with a pie server, go ahead and make a third cut, creating a second slice of pie. This will allow the first slice to release more easily.

For creamy pies, heating the blade of the knife with hot water and then drying the knife completely will help to make each pass of the knife cut more cleanly. Rinse the knife blade with hot water and dry before each subsequent slice.

Clemenza's
CANNOLI

MAKES ONE 9½-INCH DEEP-DISH PIE

WHAT YOU NEED
- Deep-Dish Single Crust (page 36), baked and cooled in a 9½-inch deep-dish pie plate
- Piping bag (see page 21) fitted with a Wilton #1M or other large star tip

Who could forget the scene in *The Godfather* with Rocco, Clemenza, and the box of cannolis? This pie is inspired by the flavors of the traditional cannoli filling, accented with orange, cinnamon, and the tang of ricotta cheese, and gilded with dark chocolate, pistachios, mini chocolate chips, and cannoli shells. You can substitute ice cream sugar cones broken into pieces for the cannoli shells.

1. MAKE THE CANNOLI SHELL DECORATION (IF USING): Cut the cannoli shells into 3 equal rings using a serrated knife and a gentle sawing motion. Dip each piece halfway into the melted semisweet chocolate and place on a sheet of wax paper or parchment set on a baking sheet. Refrigerate until the chocolate is set, at least 30 minutes or overnight.

2. ADD THE CHOCOLATE LAYER: Pour the Chocolate Ganache into the bottom of the cooled pie crust. Refrigerate until firm, about 1 hour.

recipe continues

INGREDIENT	VOLUME	WEIGHT (STANDARD)	WEIGHT (METRIC)
CANNOLI SHELL DECORATION (optional)			
Cannoli shells (full size, not miniature) (see headnote)	3 shells		
Semisweet chocolate, melted		3 ounces	85 grams
CHOCOLATE LAYER			
Chocolate Ganache (page 264), warm and pourable	¾ recipe		
CANNOLI CREAM FILLING			
Cream cheese, at room temperature	2 8-ounce packages	16 ounces	454 grams
Heavy cream	1½ cups	12.3 ounces	348 grams
Ricotta cheese (or homemade ricotta; see page 88)	1 cup	8.75 ounces	248 grams
Confectioners' sugar	¾ cup	3 ounces	85 grams
Salt	⅛ teaspoon		
Finely grated orange zest	1 teaspoon		
Vanilla extract	2 teaspoons		
Ground cinnamon	2 teaspoons		
TOPPING			
Chocolate Ganache (page 264), warm and pourable	1 recipe		
Pistachios, roasted and salted, coarsely chopped	½ cup	2.65 ounces	76 grams
Vanilla Whipped Cream (page 257)	½ recipe		
Miniature chocolate chips	2 tablespoons	0.75 ounce	21 grams

3. MAKE THE CANNOLI CREAM FILLING: In a large bowl and using a hand mixer (or in the bowl of a stand mixer fitted with the paddle attachment), beat the cream cheese on medium speed until smooth and creamy. Slowly add the cream while beating until the mixture is uniform. Add the ricotta, confectioners' sugar, and salt, followed by the orange zest, vanilla, and cinnamon, mixing until smooth. Spread in an even layer over the firm chocolate ganache. Refrigerate until set, about 2 hours or overnight.

4. MAKE THE TOPPING: Spread the warm Chocolate Ganache in a thin layer over the cannoli cream filling and sprinkle with the pistachios. Refrigerate until set, about 30 minutes.

5. Transfer the Vanilla Whipped Cream to the prepared piping bag. Pipe a decorative border around the edge of the pie. Sprinkle the mini chocolate chips over the whipped cream and place the chocolate-dipped cannoli shells into the whipped cream border. (Store any leftovers in the refrigerator for up to 3 days. The pistachios will be less crunchy by the second day.)

BLUE RIBBON BONUS:

Homemade Ricotta

In our opinion, homemade ricotta tastes a hundred times better than anything bought in a grocery store, and making it is easy. In a large pot, bring 2 cups/ 17 ounces/482 grams whole milk, 1 cup/ 8.2 ounces/232 grams heavy cream, and ¼ teaspoon salt to a boil. Remove it from the heat and stir in 1½ tablespoons/ 0.8 ounce/23 grams distilled white vinegar. Let sit for 90 seconds undisturbed. Transfer the mixture to a sieve lined with two layers of damp cheesecloth set over a bowl. Drain for 30 minutes. Scrape the cheese into a container and refrigerate until cold, at least 2 hours. Discard the liquid. You will need 1 cup/8.75 ounces/248 grams of this cheese for the cannoli cream filling (page 87). In a sealed container, the ricotta will keep in refrigerator for about 2 weeks.

KING
Fluffernutter

MAKES ONE 9½-INCH DEEP-DISH PIE

WHAT YOU NEED

• Deep-Dish Single Crust (page 36), baked and cooled in a 9½-inch deep-dish pie plate
• Piping bag (see page 21) fitted with a Wilton #1M or other large star tip (optional)

The flavors in this pie are inspired by two classic sandwiches—the Elvis and the fluffernutter. The Elvis sandwich is a combination of peanut butter, banana slices, and bacon that was reportedly a favorite of the king of rock 'n roll, Elvis Presley. The fluffernutter is a peanut butter and marshmallow creme sandwich. This creamy pie combines all of these—a peanut-studded peanut butter mousse topped with sliced fresh bananas, a banana-infused cream, and a crown of marshmallow-y brown sugar meringue. Before serving, the pie is sprinkled with chopped slices of crisp bacon deliciousness.

1. MAKE THE CANDIED BACON TOPPING: Preheat the oven to 400°F. Arrange the bacon slices on an oven-safe metal rack set inside an aluminum foil–lined sheet pan. Sprinkle the bacon evenly with the brown sugar, then place in the oven to bake until deep golden brown and crisp, 20 to 25 minutes (the bacon will crisp up once it begins to cool). Transfer the bacon to a plate lined with a double layer of paper towels to cool, then dice it into ½-inch pieces. (The chopped bacon can be stored in an airtight container in the refrigerator for up to 2 days.)

2. START THE BANANA PUDDING CREAM: Peel and slice 2 bananas into 1-inch chunks. In a small saucepan, bring the milk and 1 cup/8.2 ounces/ 232 grams of cream to a boil with the banana chunks. When the mixture boils, remove the saucepan from the heat immediately and let it cool completely before refrigerating until cold, at least 1 hour or overnight.

3. Pour the banana mixture through a fine-mesh sieve into a bowl (don't press on the bananas; discard them after straining). Transfer the strained mixture to a measuring cup. Add enough additional cream to bring the mixture to 2 cups total, then pour into a medium saucepan.

recipe continues

INGREDIENT	VOLUME	WEIGHT (STANDARD)	WEIGHT (METRIC)
CANDIED BACON TOPPING			
Thick-sliced bacon	about 4 slices	3 ounces	85 grams
Light brown sugar, lightly packed	1 tablespoon	0.45 ounce	13 grams
BANANA PUDDING CREAM			
Bananas, yellow all over, with some brown spots (weighed after peeling)	4 medium	14 ounces	400 grams
Whole milk	1 cup	8.5 ounces	242 grams
Heavy cream	1⅓ cups plus up to ¾ cup more, as needed	10.9 ounces plus up to 6.15 ounces more	309 grams plus up to 174 grams more
Cornstarch	¼ cup	1.05 ounces	30 grams
Granulated sugar	½ cup plus 1 tablespoon	4.05 ounces	115 grams
Salt	¼ teaspoon		
Eggs	2 large		
Unsalted butter, cut into 4 pieces	4 tablespoons	2 ounces	55 grams
Vanilla extract	1 teaspoon		
Fresh lemon juice	2 teaspoons		

INGREDIENT	VOLUME	WEIGHT (STANDARD)	WEIGHT (METRIC)
PEANUT BUTTER MOUSSE			
Cream cheese, at room temperature	½ 8-ounce package	4 ounces	113 grams
Confectioners' sugar	½ cup	2 ounces	57 grams
Salt	⅛ teaspoon		
Creamy peanut butter	½ cup	4.75 ounces	135 grams
Heavy cream	½ cup	4.1 ounces	116 grams
Roasted salted peanuts, chopped	⅓ cup	1.35 ounces	38 grams
BROWN SUGAR MERINGUE			
Egg whites	3 large		
Light brown sugar, lightly packed	⅔ cup	4.65 ounces	133 grams
Salt	⅛ teaspoon		
Vanilla extract	½ teaspoon		

4. Whisk the cornstarch into the banana-milk mixture. Whisk in the granulated sugar, salt, and eggs. Over medium heat, bring the mixture to a gentle boil, whisking constantly to prevent the mixture from sticking on the bottom. Reduce the heat to medium low and continue gently boiling the mixture until it thickens, whisking constantly, for about 1 minute.

5. Remove the pan from the heat and whisk in the butter and vanilla. Strain the mixture through a (clean) fine-mesh sieve into a medium bowl. The mixture is thick so you might need to press it through the sieve. Press plastic wrap on top of the mixture and refrigerate until cold, at least 3 hours or up to 1 day.

6. MAKE THE PEANUT BUTTER MOUSSE: In a small mixing bowl, beat the cream cheese in a large bowl with an electric mixer until smooth, about 30 seconds. Beat in the confectioners' sugar, salt, and peanut butter until combined.

7. In a separate bowl, whip the cream in a medium bowl on medium-high speed until it holds stiff peaks, 1 to 3 minutes. Fold the whipped cream into the peanut butter mixture. Fold in the chopped peanuts, then spread this mixture evenly over the bottom of the cooled crust. Refrigerate for 1 hour.

8. FINISH THE BANANA PUDDING CREAM: Whip the remaining ⅓ cup/ 2.7 ounces/77 grams cream in a small bowl on medium-high speed until it holds soft peaks. Rapidly stir the cold banana cream mixture with a spoon or electric mixer. It may seem a little chunky—that's okay for now. Fold the whipped cream into the banana filling until no streaks of whipped cream are visible (the mixture should be smooth and creamy).

9. Slice the 2 remaining bananas into ¼- to ½-inch slices and place them in a medium bowl. Toss the bananas with the lemon juice, and drain off any pooled lemon juice in the bottom of the bowl.

10. Evenly spread ½ cup of the banana pudding cream over the peanut butter mousse. Arrange the banana slices in a single layer on top of the cream. Spread the rest of the cream into an even layer over the banana slices. Refrigerate the pie.

11. **MAKE THE BROWN SUGAR MERINGUE:** Combine the egg whites, brown sugar, and salt in the bowl of a stand mixer. Place the bowl over a pot of simmering water to create a water bath, making sure that the bottom of the bowl does not touch the water. Cook the egg white mixture over the simmering water, whisking constantly, until it reaches 160°F on an instant-read thermometer; the mixture will be very frothy and will increase in volume.

12. Transfer the bowl to a stand mixer fitted with the whisk attachment. Beat the mixture on medium-high speed until it holds stiff peaks and the outside of the bowl is completely cool, about 10 minutes. Beat in the vanilla. Spread or pipe the meringue over the top of the pie. Just before serving, sprinkle the candied bacon over the top of the pie. (Store any leftovers in the refrigerator for up to 2 days.)

The NEW FRUIT PIES

While some fruits, like bananas and raisins, are available year-round in the grocery store, others have such a limited window of availability. Grab seasonal items, like rhubarb and Italian prune plums, when they are available and at their peak to make some of the best fruit pies you've ever had. That limited season is often not enough for us. You can extend that season even further by vacuum sealing these fruits in exact pie portion quantities and freezing them so you can enjoy them year-round too. These recipes use technology to optimize flavor and texture from what is often considered to be the most humble and rustic dessert— the fruit pie. Armed with your immersion circulator and your new appreciation for sous vide pies, you'll be able to coax peak performance out of your summer fruits and enjoy a fresh blueberry pie, even if there is a foot of snow on the ground outside.

CRAZZBERRY

MAKES ONE 9½-INCH DEEP-DISH PIE

WHAT YOU NEED

- Pie dough for a Deep-Dish Double Crust (page 36)
- 9½-inch deep-dish pie plate
- Fondant impression mat (optional; see Blue Ribbon Bonus, page 96)
- Vacuum sealer
- Immersion circulator
- Pie crust shield or foil (see page 19)

Most people see cranberries just once per year—in a single course, of a single meal, as a side dish to accompany a roast turkey. We don't think that is sufficient airtime for this beautiful little berry. In addition to the intense fuchsia-on-steroids color they bring to a plate, they are tart, flavorful, and a great source of pectin—all ideal qualities for a pie fruit. In this pie, they are paired with raspberries and accented with hints of orange and clove. Cranberries and raspberries both freeze very well, allowing you to make this pie as a cranberry encore for your table any time of the year.

1. Use an immersion circulator to heat a water bath to 150°F (see sous vide instructions on page 28). Place 6¾ cups/24 ounces/680 grams of the cranberries in a vacuum-sealable bag along with ⅔ cup/4.65 ounces/133 grams of the sugar. Vacuum-seal the bag. Cook the cranberries sous vide in the water bath for 1 hour. Remove the bag and snip a small section off the corner of the bag with kitchen scissors. The hole should be smaller than a cranberry to prevent cranberries from coming out of the bag. Pour the liquid released from the bag into a medium saucepan. Place the bag with the cooked cranberries in a bowl in the refrigerator to cool completely.

2. Roll out the first disc of dough to a ⅛-inch thickness (page 42) and place in a 9½-inch deep-dish pie plate. Place the pie plate with the untrimmed pie dough in the refrigerator.

3. Into that saucepan with the cranberry liquid, add the remaining 1¾ cups/6 ounces/170 grams of cranberries, and the remaining 1⅔ cups/11.65 ounces/333 grams of sugar along with the raspberries, orange zest, orange juice, salt, cloves, and cornstarch. Stir with a rubber

recipe continues

INGREDIENT	VOLUME	WEIGHT (STANDARD)	WEIGHT (METRIC)
Cranberries, fresh (picked through for stems and twigs, soft berries discarded) or frozen	8½ cups	30 ounces	850 grams
Sugar	2⅓ cups	16.3 ounces	466 grams
Raspberries, fresh or frozen	1¼ cups	6 ounces	170 grams
Finely grated orange zest	1 tablespoon		
Fresh orange juice	1 teaspoon		
Salt	⅛ teaspoon		
Ground cloves	⅛ teaspoon		
Cornstarch	1 tablespoon	0.25 ounce	8 grams
Raspberry emulsion (optional)	½ teaspoon		
Egg yolk	1 large		
Heavy cream	1 tablespoon	0.5 ounce	15 grams

spatula until the ingredients are all moistened and bring the mixture to a boil over medium heat (the cranberries will start to pop). Keep stirring with the rubber spatula, pressing lightly on the berries until it seems that they are mostly popped, the sugar is dissolved, and the liquid is thickened slightly, about 10 minutes.

4. Pour the mixture into a blender and blend on low to medium speed until smooth. Strain the mixture through a fine-mesh sieve back into the saucepan (or a clean bowl if you don't mind having to do extra dishes) to remove the raspberry seeds. Press on the contents to make sure you get as much of the liquid as possible. Fold in the chilled cranberries from the refrigerator along with the raspberry emulsion, if using (for added raspberry flavor). Pour this mixture into the bottom of the pie that has been chilling in the refrigerator.

5. Roll out the dough for the top crust to a ⅛-inch thickness and drape it on top of the filled pie. Press together the bottom and top crusts, rotating the pie as you go, until the crust is completely sealed. Trim the excess and roll the edge under. Crimp it decoratively (see page 24) and place the pie in the freezer for 20 minutes. Adjust an oven rack to the bottom position and heat the oven to 425°F.

6. In a small bowl, stir the egg yolk with the cream until combined. Brush this egg wash over the top surface of the pie.

7. With a sharp knife, cut 3 to 5 evenly spaced 1-inch vents in the top crust to allow for steam to escape and for expansion of the crust. Place the pie on the bottom oven rack and immediately lower the temperature to 400°F. After 15 minutes add a pie crust shield to protect the crust edges and rotate the pie a quarter turn. Bake an additional 40 minutes, rotating the pie another quarter turn halfway through to minimize the effects of any hot spots in your oven. At this point the pie should be golden brown on top.

8. Remove the pie from the oven, place on a cooling rack, and allow several hours for it to cool to room temperature before slicing. (Leftovers can be stored, covered, at room temperature for up to 3 days.)

THE GUYS TALK PIES: *Sweetie Pies*

Did you realize that this recipe for Crazzberry pie calls for over a pound of sugar? Seems a bit excessive, don't you think? Actually, no! This pie is not too sweet at all because these fruits are naturally quite tart. You really do need this amount of sugar to bring the flavors into a pleasant balance. And remember—each slice only has a fraction of that sugar.

BLUE RIBBON BONUS:

Using an Impression Mat to Decorate a Top Crust

On a silicone mat, roll out the dough for the top crust into a circle, ⅛ inch thick. Place a well-floured fondant impression mat (any pretty design can be used that is large enough to cover the dough circle) on top of the dough and roll across the mat with your rolling pin, applying a steady, even pressure. Slide the silicone mat with the dough and impression mat onto the back of a half sheet pan and place the pan in the refrigerator until the dough is stiff, about 15 minutes. The impression mat can now be carefully peeled off, revealing the decorative pattern for your top crust, which can be kept in the refrigerator until you are ready to assemble your pie as described. When brushing the egg wash (regular or with added food color; see page 26) over the top surface of the pie, follow the pattern, making sure that the impressed areas are all filled with the egg wash. Place the pie back in the freezer for 10 minutes before baking. When the pie has baked, the egg wash that settled into the dough grooves from the impression mat will display the decorative pattern.

Spiced
APPLE
CIDER

MAKES ONE 9½-INCH DEEP-DISH PIE

WHAT YOU NEED
- Pie dough for a Deep-Dish Double Crust (page 36)
- 9½-inch deep-dish pie plate
- Cake portion marker
- Pie crust shield or foil (see page 19)

This blue ribbon–winning pie is thickened solely with the power of fruit. For the ultimate in apple flavor and texture, we call for two types of apples: one that holds its shape when baked (such as Granny Smith) and one that melts away into the background (we like McIntosh). Like a row of backup singers, the golden raisins, apricots, and candied ginger all play a supporting role in making the apples taste more apple-y while providing structure to the filling. As an added bonus, the whole house smells amazing while this is cooking.

1. Preheat the oven to 325°F. Add the raisins, apricots, ginger, lemon zest, and lemon juice to the bowl of a food processor and puree to make a coarse paste.

2. Place a large roasting pan (the one you would use for your Thanksgiving turkey) on the stovetop over medium heat. Melt the butter in the pan, then add the pureed dried fruits, brown sugar, cinnamon, nutmeg, ginger, cloves, salt, apple cider, and Calvados. Stir the mixture with a rubber spatula over medium heat until it is simmering, about 10 minutes. Add the apples and stir until the mixture returns to a gentle simmer.

3. Place the roasting pan in the oven and stir every 30 minutes, for a total of about 90 minutes. The goal is for the filling to be reduced

recipe continues

INGREDIENT	VOLUME	WEIGHT (STANDARD)	WEIGHT (METRIC)
Golden raisins	1¾ cups	8.5 ounces	240 grams
Dried apricots	1 cup	5.6 ounces	160 grams
Crystallized ginger	¼ cup	1.4 ounces	40 grams
Finely grated lemon zest	1 tablespoon		
Fresh lemon juice	3 tablespoons	1.5 ounces	43 grams
Unsalted butter	8 tablespoons	4 ounces	113 grams
Light brown sugar, lightly packed	1 cup	7 ounces	200 grams
Ground cinnamon	1 teaspoon		
Ground nutmeg	½ teaspoon		
Ground ginger	½ teaspoon		
Ground cloves	¼ teaspoon		
Kosher salt	½ teaspoon		
Apple cider or juice	2 cups	17 ounces	484 grams
Calvados or other apple brandy	½ cup	4 ounces	113 grams
Granny Smith apples, about 6 medium, peeled, cored, and sliced into thin wedges	8 cups (sliced)	32 ounces	907 grams
McIntosh apples, about 5 medium, peeled, cored, and sliced into thin wedges	6 cups (sliced)	24 ounces	680 grams
Egg yolk	1 large		

to 8 cups. Some of the apples will have melted into a thick brown applesauce while others will become soft-tender and stay mostly intact (when you drag a rubber spatula across the bottom of the pan, it should leave a trail). Remove the pan from the oven.

4. When cool enough to handle, transfer the filling to an airtight container and refrigerate until you are ready to assemble the pie. (The filling can be prepared several days in advance.)

5. Following the instructions on page 42, roll out the dough for the top crust to a ⅛-inch thickness and then transfer it to a sheet of parchment. Using a cake portion marker (see page 18) like you would a cookie cutter, cut 18 equally spaced lines like the spokes of a wheel into the top crust (you could accomplish this feat with a ruler, knife, and a protractor like some kind of high school geometry–home economics class mash-up). Using a pizza wheel (or butter knife), extend the cuts to the outer edges of the dough circle. The top crust should now look like a sun with the central 2-inch circle surrounded by rays of dough.

6. One by one, flip over each of the 18 "rays" of dough, placing it back down in the same place but with a single twist (see page 34). You can flip them all in the same direction or alternate directions. Both are pretty patterns. Place the top crust in the freezer while rolling out the bottom.

7. Roll out the bottom pie dough to a ⅛-inch thickness. Fit the dough into a 9½-inch deep-dish pie plate. Pour the refrigerated filling into the pie, smoothing with an offset spatula. Remove the top crust from the freezer (it should be stiff and relatively easy to handle). Slide the top crust off the parchment onto the top of the pie.

8. Press the bottom and top crust edges together, rotating the pie as you go (a cake-decorating or lazy Susan–style turntable works great for this). The warmth from your fingers will start to soften the top crust. Keep rotating and pressing until the top and bottom are malleable and sealed. Trim the excess to about ½ inch beyond the edge of the pie plate and roll the edge under. Crimp it decoratively (see page 24) and place the pie in the freezer for 30 minutes. While the pie is chilling, adjust an oven rack to the lowest position and preheat the oven to 425°F.

9. In a small bowl, stir the egg yolk and 1 teaspoon water together until evenly combined. Brush this egg wash over the center of the pie and along the twisted "rays" of dough.

10. Place the pie on the oven rack and immediately lower the oven temperature to 400°F. Bake for 15 minutes; pale golden spots should be starting to appear on the crust. Rotate the pie, adding a pie crust shield to protect the edges from getting too dark. Bake an additional 40 minutes, until the crust is richly browned. Remove the pie from the oven and allow it to cool to room temperature before slicing.

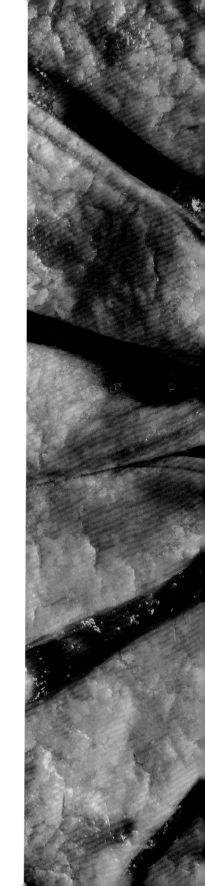

Aunt Melba's
PEACH

MAKES ONE 9½-INCH DEEP-DISH PIE

WHAT YOU NEED

- Pie dough for a Deep-Dish Double Crust (page 36)
- 9½-inch deep-dish pie plate
- Pie crust shield or foil (see page 19)
- Vanilla ice cream, for serving (optional)

Full disclosure: neither of us actually has an Aunt Melba. Rather, the combination of peaches, raspberries, caramel-y turbinado sugar, and vanilla are inspired by the classic peach Melba dessert. We sometimes name new recipes after fictitious relatives when entering them in contests to give them an air of authenticity. This fairly traditional lattice-topped pie was certainly a good candidate for such attribution. Does it help? Maybe or maybe not, but it certainly keeps us entertained!

1. Roll out the first disc of dough (the larger of the 2 discs) to a ⅛-inch thickness (see page 42) and place in the deep-dish pie plate. Place the pie plate with the untrimmed pie dough in the refrigerator.

2. Roll out the second disc of dough into a rectangle approximately 16 by 10 inches, 1/16 inch thick. If you have rolled it on a silicone mat, transfer the dough to a piece of parchment. Using a ruler, cut the dough into 1-inch-wide strips. Slide the parchment with the cut strips onto the back of a half sheet pan and place the pan in the refrigerator until the strips are firm, about 15 minutes.

3. Weave the dough strips into a lattice (see page 27) and place back in the refrigerator until you are ready to assemble the pie.

4. Thaw the peaches in a colander, collecting the juices in a large bowl. This amount of peaches should produce about 2¼ cups of liquid. Once the peaches have completely thawed, set aside ¼ cup of the peach juice and pour the rest into a medium saucepan. Bring that liquid to a boil over medium-high heat, and simmer until it is reduced to ¾ cup, about 15 minutes. (If you are not very good at estimating volumes by eye, you may need to pour your reduced liquid into a glass measuring cup to confirm). The reduced juice will be thick, dark, and syrupy and can be removed from the heat.

recipe continues

INGREDIENT	VOLUME	WEIGHT (STANDARD)	WEIGHT (METRIC)
Peaches, peeled, sliced into ½-inch wedges, and frozen (from approximately 4 pounds whole fresh peaches)	8 cups	48 ounces	1,361 grams
Freeze-dried raspberries (see Sources, page 265)	1 scant cup	0.5 ounce	15 grams
Turbinado sugar	¾ cup	5.25 ounces	150 grams
Salt	⅛ teaspoon		
Tapioca starch	2 tablespoons	0.5 ounce	15 grams
Cornstarch	2 tablespoons	0.55 ounce	15 grams
Vanilla extract	1 teaspoon		
Egg white	1 large		
Heavy cream	1 tablespoon	0.5 ounce	15 grams

5. Grind the freeze-dried raspberries in a spice grinder or small food processor until reduced to a powder with seeds. Use a fine-mesh sieve to remove the seeds and add this powder with the sugar and salt to the reduced peach liquid, stirring to dissolve the sugar.

6. Stir the tapioca starch and cornstarch into the reserved ¼ cup peach juice and then add it to the saucepan with the reduced peach juice mixture. Bring the mixture back to a boil; after a few minutes, you'll notice streaks of thickened juice in the liquid—don't worry, this is the tapioca starch thickening first (tapioca starch thickens at a slightly lower temperature than the cornstarch). Keep stirring; once the liquid comes to a boil, the cornstarch will thicken too and the liquid will transform from thin and cloudy into a rich, clearer dark gel. Remove from the heat and fold in the raw peaches and vanilla. Transfer this mixture into the bottom of the pie that has been chilling in the fridge.

7. Place the completed lattice from the refrigerator on top of the pie; the heat from the peaches will start to soften the lattice. With the pie on a turntable (or on a flat work surface), start pressing the bottom and top crusts together, rotating the pie as you go. Keep rotating and pressing until the top and bottom are malleable and sealed (don't try to crimp too-cold dough—it will crack). Trim the excess and roll the edge under. Crimp it decoratively (see page 24) and place the pie in the freezer for 20 minutes while heating the oven to 425°F with the oven rack placed in the lowest position.

8. Lightly beat the egg white with the cream until combined but not frothy. Brush this egg wash over the top surface of the pie. Place the pie on the lowest rack of the oven. Immediately lower the temperature to 400°F. After 15 minutes, add a pie crust shield to protect the edges and then rotate the pie. Bake until the pie is golden brown and the pie liquid starts to barely bubble at the edges, about an additional 40 minutes, rotating the pie again halfway to brown evenly.

9. Remove the pie from the oven, place on a cooling rack, and allow it to cool to room temperature before slicing. The pie is great by itself, but also pairs very well with a scoop of vanilla ice cream. (Leftovers can be stored, covered, at room temperature for up to 3 days.)

THE GUYS TALK PIES: *Fillings*

Most recipes for traditionally baked pies do not call for precooking the fillings; the fruits and thickeners go into the crust completely raw. For those pies, it is essential to bake until the pie is bubbling in the center to make sure that the released liquids will have reached the gelling temperature of the thickener. Ideally, the filling will start to bubble at the same time the crust is finished baking. Depending on the amount of liquid released from the fruits, there may sometimes be a mismatch with the amount of thickener needed, which can result in either a gluey or soupy pie filling. Likewise, if the volume of the liquid is too great, the crust may be finished and starting to burn before the filling has thickened. By reducing the liquid and pre-thickening the filling—as is done here with Aunt Melba's Peach and The Apple (page 112)—you can reduce some of that baking-time uncertainty and keep your meticulously assembled top crusts looking pretty.

GUAVABERRY APPLE

MAKES ONE 9-INCH PIE

WHAT YOU NEED

- Pie dough for a Standard Single Crust (page 35)
- 9-inch standard pie plate
- Pie crust shield or foil (see page 19)

Guavaberries are little reddish-purple tropical fruits—no relation to guavas. We tried really hard to find a commercial source of guavaberry preserves, but came up empty-handed (we get ours from Paul's mom, and no, we won't give you her address)—which is why this is a four-star ingredient recipe rather than a three-star; most of you who have never even heard of a guavaberry are *really* unlikely to find any. *(What? This is an outrage! What kind of cookbook is this anyway?)* Have no fear! You can still make this pie without guavaberries; just use black currant preserves instead.

1. PARTIALLY BLIND-BAKE THE CRUST: Follow the instructions on page 47. The pie will bake longer after the filling is added, so it should not be completely browned at this point. Remove the pie dish from the oven, set it on a wire cooling rack, and remove the foil or parchment and pie weights. Keep the oven at 350°F.

2. MAKE THE FILLING: Melt the butter over medium heat in a large pan with a lid (such as a 5-quart Dutch oven). Using a rubber spatula, stir in the sugar, allspice, cinnamon, salt, and cloves until fully moistened. Add the apples and stir until they are coated with the butter mixture. Cover the pot, reduce the heat to low, and cook until the apples are soft and release some liquid, 20 minutes, stirring midway through. If, after 20 minutes, the apples are still firm, put the cover back on, turn the heat up a bit, and keep checking every 5 minutes until they have started to soften.

recipe continues

INGREDIENT	VOLUME	WEIGHT (STANDARD)	WEIGHT (METRIC)
FILLING			
Unsalted butter	2 tablespoons	1 ounce	28 grams
Sugar	¼ cup	1.75 ounces	50 grams
Ground allspice	¼ teaspoon		
Ground cinnamon	⅛ teaspoon		
Salt	⅛ teaspoon		
Ground cloves	pinch		
Golden Delicious apples, about 3 pounds, peeled, cored, and sliced into thin wedges	10 cups (sliced)	40 ounces	1,134 grams
Guavaberry (or black currant) preserves	½ cup	5.4 ounces	153 grams
Boiled apple cider syrup (see page 265)	2 tablespoons	1.25 ounces	36 grams
Tapioca starch	1 tablespoon	0.25 ounce	8 grams
Cornstarch	1 tablespoon	0.25 ounce	8 grams
CRUNCHY TOPPING			
Unsalted butter	5 tablespoons	2.5 ounces	71 grams
Ground cinnamon	⅛ teaspoon		
Sugar	⅓ cup	2.3 ounces	65 grams
Salt	pinch		
Panko breadcrumbs (unseasoned)	1¼ cups	2.5 ounces	71 grams

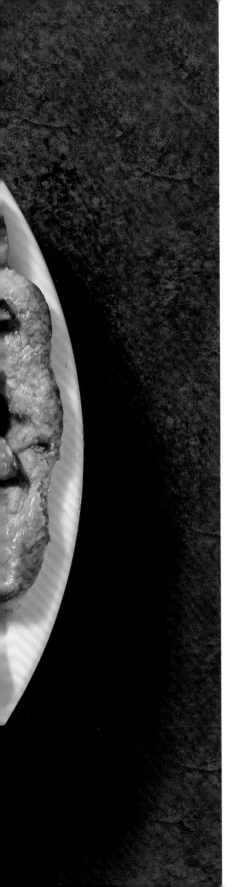

3. While the apples are cooking, puree the guavaberry (or black currant) preserves in a small blender or food processor. Add the boiled cider, tapioca starch, and cornstarch and blend until they are dissolved.

4. Using a large slotted spoon, transfer the apples to a bowl, leaving the liquid in the pot. Add the guavaberry mixture to the pot and increase the heat to medium-high. Using the rubber spatula, keep stirring the mixture until it has thickened and is just starting to boil. Fold the apple slices back into this thickened mixture; set aside while preparing the topping.

5. MAKE THE TOPPING: Melt the butter in a small bowl. Stir in the cinnamon, sugar, and salt. The sugar will remain mostly undissolved; that is okay. Add the panko and stir until all of the crumbs are coated with the sugar mixture.

6. FILL THE CRUST AND BAKE: Pour the apple filling into the warm pie shell. Press down on the filling using the rubber spatula or a small offset spatula, creating a flat surface for the topping. Using your fingers, sprinkle the panko topping in an even layer across the surface of the pie. Cover the edges of the pie with a pie crust shield and bake on the middle rack of the oven until the topping is just starting to toast slightly, about 20 minutes.

7. Remove the pie from the oven, place on a cooling rack, and allow the pie to cool completely, at least 4 hours, before serving. (Leftovers can be stored, covered, at room temperature for up to 3 days.)

Maple
BLUEBERRY

MAKES ONE 9½-INCH DEEP-DISH PIE

WHAT YOU NEED

- Pie dough for a Deep-Dish Double Crust (page 36)
- 9½-inch deep-dish pie plate
- Immersion circulator in a water bath
- Vacuum sealer
- Wood-grain impression mat (optional; see Blue Ribbon Bonus, page 108)
- Pie crust shield or foil (see page 19)

Think of fresh blueberry pancakes covered in maple syrup and you will have the inspiration for this pie. The blueberries are precooked in a vacuum-sealed bag, immersed in a water bath, and heated using the sous vide technique (see page 28). The use of this precision cooking method allows you to heat the blueberries to the perfect temperature that alters the natural pectin in the berries, keeping them firm but just cooked enough and bursting with fresh berry flavor. For an added bonus, we use a silicone impression mat (see page 27) to create a wood-grain pattern in the lattice to echo the origin of the maple syrup used in the filling.

1. DIVIDE THE PIE DOUGH INTO 3 DISCS: Use about 60% of the dough to create 1 disc and then divide the remaining dough into 2 equal discs. If you are using a scale (recommended!), the first piece should be 15 ounces/425 grams and the other two pieces should each be 5.5 ounces/156 grams.

2. Roll out the largest disc to a 15-inch circle that is ⅛ inch thick and place in the deep-dish pie plate (don't trim the edges). Place the pie plate in the refrigerator.

3. Roll out the first of the 2 small discs of dough into an approximate 8 by 11-inch rectangle that is 1/16 inch thick. Place the rolled-out dough on a piece of parchment. To make a simple lattice top, using a ruler and a pizza wheel or knife, cut the dough into the first 2 lattice strips that are each about 3½ by 11 inches. Place these 2 strips in the refrigerator until you are ready to assemble your pie. Repeat with the remaining piece of dough.

recipe continues

INGREDIENT	VOLUME	WEIGHT (STANDARD)	WEIGHT (METRIC)
Blueberries, fresh	6 cups	36 ounces	1,021 grams
Granny Smith apple	1 medium	6.5 ounces	184 grams
Finely ground quick-cooking tapioca, such as Minute	2 tablespoons plus 1 teaspoon	0.85 ounce	24 grams
Sugar	¼ cup plus 3 tablespoons	3 ounces	85 grams
Salt	⅛ teaspoon		
Ground cinnamon	⅛ teaspoon		
Maple extract	1 teaspoon		
Fresh lemon juice	1 tablespoon	0.5 ounces	14 grams
Maple syrup	¼ cup plus 2 teaspoons	3.5 ounces	100 grams
Egg yolk	1 large		
Heavy cream	1 tablespoon	0.5 ounce	15 grams

4. To prepare the filling, place the blueberries onto a half sheet pan and put them in the freezer until frozen (at least a couple of hours). Spreading them out as much as possible allows them to freeze individually rather than in one large clump. (If you don't have room in your freezer for a sheet pan, make sure to dry them really well and freeze them in a smaller container.)

5. Set up the water bath for your immersion circulator and start heating the water to 150°F (see sous vide instructions on page 28). Transfer the frozen blueberries to a vacuum-sealable bag. Peel the apple and grate it using the coarse holes of a box grater; squeeze the grated apple to remove as much of the juice as possible, and then add the apple to the blueberries using your fingers to evenly disperse. With the bag standing upright, add the tapioca, sugar, salt, cinnamon, maple extract, lemon juice, and maple syrup. Gently shake the bag to disperse the contents and then vacuum seal it shut.

Cook the blueberries sous vide in the water bath for 1 hour. Remove the bag and place it on a kitchen towel to cool for 5 minutes on your countertop. Cut the bag open and pour the blueberry mixture into the chilled pie shell, squeezing out every bit of juice from the bag. (At this point the berries will still appear intact, and the released dark blueberry juices may still appear disturbingly thin; that's okay, they will thicken up.)

6. Place the lattice strips from the refrigerator on top of the pie, forming a simple 4-plank lattice. The heat from the blueberries, along with the warmth from your fingers, will start to soften the lattice. Start pressing the bottom and top crust edges together, rotating the pie as you go. Keep rotating and pressing until the top and bottom is malleable and sealed. Trim the excess and roll the edge under. Crimp it decoratively (see page 24) and place the pie in the freezer for 20 minutes; adjust an oven rack to the lowest position, and preheat the oven to 425°F.

7. Stir the egg yolk and the cream together until evenly combined. Brush the egg wash over the top surface of the pie. Place the pie on the bottom oven rack and immediately lower the temperature to 400°F. After 15 minutes, add a pie shield to protect the edges and rotate the pie. Bake an additional 40 minutes, rotating the pie again halfway through to brown evenly. The blueberry liquid should be just barely starting to bubble at the edges.

8. Remove the pie from the oven, place on a cooling rack, and cool to room temperature before slicing. (Leftovers can be stored, covered, at room temperature for up to 3 days.)

BLUE RIBBON BONUS:
Making Wood-Grain Lattice

In Step 3, a wood-grain design may be added to the lattice using a fondant impression mat (see "Equipment," page 18). Dust the impression mat with flour and place it on top of the rolled-out dough on the parchment with the wood-grain surface facing the dough. Carefully roll the rolling pin across the full length of the dough using even pressure. Slide the parchment, dough, and impression mat onto the back of a half sheet pan and place it in the refrigerator for about 15 minutes. Once the dough is firm, peel off the impression mat. Using a ruler and a pizza wheel, slice the dough in half lengthwise, producing the first 2 lattice strips and refrigerate as described until you are ready to assemble your pie. Repeat this process with the second small disc of rolled-out dough. Assemble the pie as described in Step 7. When brushing the egg wash over the top surface of the pie (Step 8), follow the wood-grain pattern, making sure that the impressed areas are all filled with the egg wash. When the pie has baked, the egg wash that settled into the wood grain will have browned, making it appear that you have covered your pie with a lattice made from 4 planks of wood.

Note: You can substitute maple sugar for the granulated sugar in both the pie dough and the filling. You can further reinforce the flavors in this pie by adding ⅛ teaspoon of cinnamon to the pie dough.

Shaking Up
SHAKER
LEMON

MAKES ONE 9½-INCH DEEP-DISH PIE

WHAT YOU NEED
- Pie dough for a Deep-Dish Single Crust (page 36)
- 9½-inch deep-dish pie plate
- Vacuum sealer
- Immersion circulator (optional)
- Pie crust shield or foil (see page 19)

This pie is for all of you marmalade lovers out there. It uses the whole lemon—juice, zest, and pith. Actually, the seeds are removed, so it is *almost* the whole lemon. It is a complex combination of sweet, sour, and bitter flavors in two layers; a rich custard and a light, creamy topping. It is also a pie that can be made using the sous vide technique, even if you don't have an immersion circulator, converting the equipment rating for this recipe from a 3 star to a 1 star. Note that you should stock up on Meyer lemons during the brief season when they are available—whether that's one day or up to many months before making the pie.

1. To start the filling, slice off and discard the pointy ends of the lemons. Cut the whole lemons into approximately 1-inch pieces. Carefully inspect and remove seeds using the tip of a paring knife. Place the lemon chunks (including peel and pith) into the bowl of a food processor and puree until finely chopped, about 1 minute. You should have 2 cups/20 ounces/567 grams of lemon puree.

2. Scoop equal portions of the lemon puree into 2 vacuum-sealable bags. Fold the tops over so they do not leak, but don't seal them yet. Place them in the freezer for at least 2 hours. Once frozen, add the granulated sugar and salt to one of the bags and vacuum-seal them both. (Sealing the bags after the fruit has frozen helps prevent the juice from leaking out during the sealing process.) Place both bags in the freezer until you are ready to make the pie (this can be done several months before you plan on making the pie).

3. Set up the water bath for your immersion circulator (see the sous vide instructions on page 28) and start heating the water to 195°F. Or, because the cooking temperature for this filling is so close to the boiling point of water, you can substitute a stockpot filled halfway with water. On the stovetop, bring the water to a boil and then maintain it at a gentle simmer.

recipe continues

INGREDIENT	VOLUME	WEIGHT (STANDARD)	WEIGHT (METRIC)
Meyer lemons	4 medium	21 ounces	595 grams
Granulated sugar	2 cups	14 ounces	397 grams
Salt	¼ teaspoon		
Unsalted butter, melted	1 tablespoon	0.5 ounce	14 grams
Eggs	4 large		
Cornstarch	1 tablespoon	0.25 ounce	8 grams
Unflavored powdered gelatin	½ teaspoon		
Heavy cream	½ cup	4.1 ounces	116 grams
Confectioners' sugar	1 tablespoon	0.25 ounce	7 grams
Sweetened condensed milk	1 14-ounce can	14 ounces	397 grams

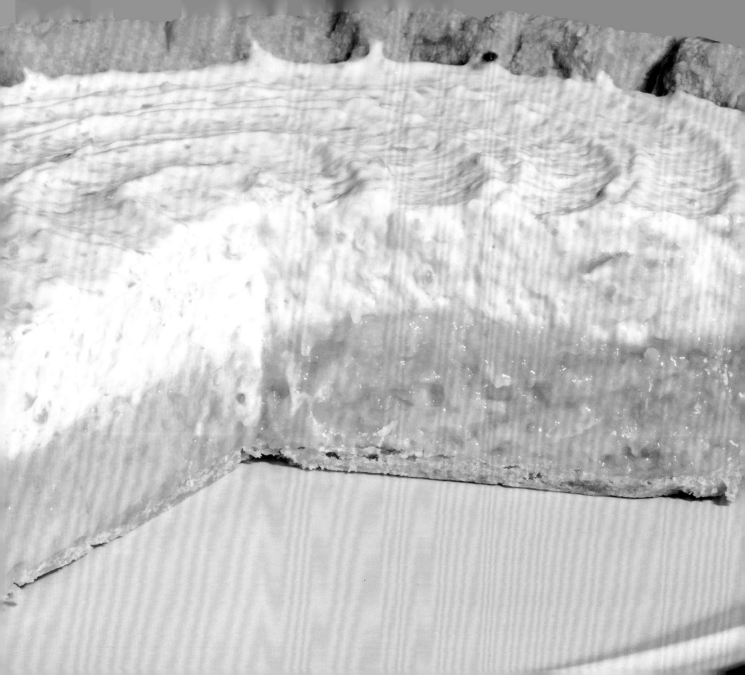

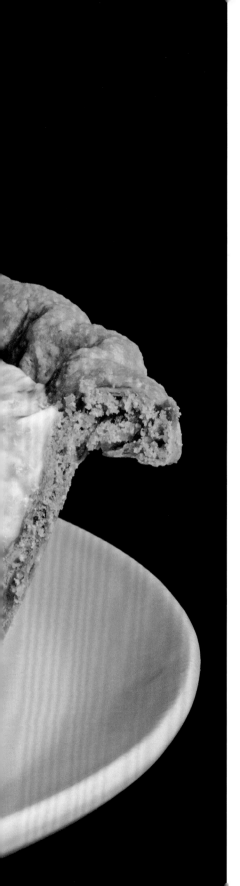

4. Place both lemon bags in the water bath for 1 hour, flipping the bags (using tongs and oven mitts or a kitchen towel) halfway through to ensure that the contents are well mixed. You may want to squish the bag with the lemon-sugar mixture a bit during the flip to ensure even mixing. (If using the stovetop method, you may need to weigh the bags down to keep them submerged—a vegetable steamer basket works well for this task.) Remove both bags from the water bath. Place the plain lemon bag in the refrigerator for later and keep the bag with the lemon-sugar mixture out to make the custard.

5. While the lemons cook, follow the instructions on page 47 to partially blind-bake the crust. The pie will bake longer after the filling is added, so it should not be completely browned at this point. Remove the pie dish from the oven, set it on a wire cooling rack, and remove the foil or parchment and pie weights. Keep the oven at 350°F.

6. In a medium bowl, whisk the melted butter, eggs, and cornstarch until incorporated. Open the vacuum-sealed bag containing the lemon-sugar mixture and use a rubber spatula to fold the cooked lemon puree into the butter mixture, making sure to squeeze out all the lemon mixture from the bag.

7. Place a pie shield on the crust to protect the edges from drips and splashes and pour the mixture into the warm pie shell. Place the pie in the oven and bake until the filling has puffed and set, about 30 minutes. Remove from the oven and cool completely on a wire cooling rack.

8. Place 2 teaspoons water in a small bowl. Sprinkle the gelatin on top and allow it to soften for 5 minutes.

9. In a medium bowl, whip the cream and confectioners' sugar on medium-high speed until it holds stiff peaks, 1 to 3 minutes. Add the condensed milk and continue to whip until incorporated. Add the reserved chilled lemon puree and whip until incorporated.

10. Microwave the small bowl of softened gelatin for 10 seconds, stirring after 5 seconds until the gelatin is just melted. Add the melted gelatin to the lemon-cream mixture and whip until incorporated. Pour the lemon-cream mixture into the pie and smooth the top. Refrigerate for at least 4 hours, until the topping has set before serving. (Leftovers can be stored in the refrigerator for up to 2 days.)

The APPLE

MAKES ONE 9½-INCH DEEP-DISH PIE

WHAT YOU NEED
- Pie dough for a Deep-Dish Double Crust (page 36)
- 9½-inch deep-dish pie plate
- Vacuum sealer
- Immersion circulator
- Pie crust shield or foil (see page 19)

Every pie book has to have a basic apple pie, but you may have already noticed that we don't exactly do *basic pies* (at least not the way our grandmothers used to). Using the sous vide method and boiling the juices before baking, we create an apple pie with a crisp crust and perfectly cooked apples cradled in a filling that is gooey but perfectly sliceable. A classic dessert made better through the use of technology and ingenuity—what could be more American? Try the green chile variation with flavors of the American Southwest for a twist on the classic.

1. Set up the water bath for your immersion circulator and heat the water to 155°F (see the sous vide instructions on page 28).

2. Peel 1 apple and grate it using the coarse holes of a box grater directly into a large vacuum-sealable bag. Peel and core the remaining apples (save all the scraps) and slice them into thin wedges. Place 48 ounces/1,361 grams of apple wedges into the vacuum bag with the grated apple. You may have a few wedges left over (snack on them while the other apples are cooking).

3. Add the lemon juice, sugar, salt, and cinnamon to the bag with the apples and vacuum-seal it shut, being careful not to lose any of the juice from the apples in the process. Gather up the apple scraps and place them in a separate vacuum bag. Vacuum-seal that one, too. Cook the apples and apple scraps sous vide in the water bath for 1 hour. Remove the bag with the apple scraps and place it on the counter to cool for a few minutes. Using oven mitts or a kitchen towel, remove the bag with the apple wedges. Cut a ¼-inch hole in the bag and pour out the liquid into a 2-cup liquid measuring cup. Once all the juice has been drained, place the bag of apples in the refrigerator until the fruit is cold, about 2 hours.

recipe continues

INGREDIENT	VOLUME	WEIGHT (STANDARD)	WEIGHT (METRIC)
Granny Smith apples	about 8 medium	4 pounds	1,814 grams
Fresh lemon juice	1 tablespoon	0.5 ounce	14 grams
Turbinado sugar	½ cup	3.5 ounces	100 grams
Salt	¼ teaspoon		
Ground cinnamon	½ teaspoon		
Cornstarch	2 tablespoons plus ¾ teaspoon	0.6 ounce	17 grams
Tapioca starch	2 tablespoons plus ¾ teaspoon	0.6 ounce	17 grams
Unsalted butter	2 tablespoons	1 ounce	28 grams
Heavy cream	1 tablespoon	0.5 ounce	15 grams
Egg white	1 large		

4. Cut a small hole in the bag with the apple scraps and squeeze additional juice into the same measuring cup with the juice from the other bag until you get 2 cups of liquid. Discard the remaining apple scraps. Cover the measuring cup with plastic wrap and allow the liquid to cool to room temperature, until you are ready to complete the pie. (The apples and apple juice can be kept in the refrigerator for up to 1 day before completing the pie.)

5. Follow the instructions on page 42 to roll out the bottom pie dough to ⅛-inch thickness. Fit the dough into a 9½-inch deep-dish pie plate. Place the pie in the refrigerator until you are ready to fill it.

6. Stir the cornstarch and tapioca starch into the cooled apple liquid. Melt the butter in a large saucepan. Using a rubber spatula, stir the apple liquid into the saucepan and bring the mixture to a boil; after a few minutes, you'll notice streaks of thickened juice in the liquid—don't worry; this is the tapioca starch thickening first (tapioca starch thickens at a slightly lower temperature than cornstarch). Keep stirring; once the liquid comes to a boil, the cornstarch will thicken as well and the liquid will transform from thin and cloudy into a rich, clearer dark gel. Remove from the heat and fold in the chilled apple wedges. Transfer this mixture to the chilled pie crust and leave at room temperature while you prepare the top crust.

7. Roll out the top crust to a ⅛-inch thickness. Place on top of the pie. Pinch the top and bottom crusts together around the edges using your thumb and fingertips. Trim off the excess. You'll want about ½ inch of crust extending beyond the edge of the pie plate. Fold/roll this flap of pie dough under itself and crimp (see page 24) around the edge of the pie. Place the pie in the freezer for 20 minutes while preheating the oven to 425°F.

8. Beat the cream and egg white together to create an egg wash. Brush the egg wash over the surface of the pie. With a sharp knife, cut 3 to 5 vents through the top crust.

9. Place the pie on the lowest rack of the oven. Immediately reduce the temperature to 400°F. After 15 minutes, add a pie crust shield to protect the edges and rotate the pie. Bake an additional 40 minutes, rotating the pie again halfway through to minimize the effects of any hot spots in your oven. At this point the pie will have puffed slightly and browned. There should also be just a hint of the gelled apple juices starting to bubble through one of the vents. Stop there.

10. Remove the pie from the oven, place on a cooling rack, and allow it to cool to room temperature, before slicing. (Leftovers can be stored, covered, at room temperature for up to 3 days.)

Variation:
GREEN CHILE APPLE

Replace the cinnamon and lemon juice with equal amounts of ground cumin and lime juice. Add 4 ounces chopped New Mexico green chiles to the vacuum bag when you add the grated apple. If you are lucky enough to have access to peeled freshly roasted chiles, please use them. If not, canned (drained) chiles are a reasonable substitute. A nice scoop of vanilla ice cream (optional) tames the mild heat of the chiles.

THE PROBLEM WITH APPLE PIE

As the apples for a pie cook, they shrink and release liquids that will, it is hoped, be absorbed and thickened by the added starch (in our recipe, that's a combination of cornstarch and tapioca starch) rather than making the crust soggy. That liquid usually needs to reach the right temperature to thicken, which ideally occurs close to the time that the crust is finished baking but is not yet burnt. No wonder pie baking stresses some people out! This recipe aims to solve these problems. By precooking the apples using the sous vide method, you'll find they will be evenly and perfectly cooked, not mushy. Also, by controlling the exact amount of liquid in the matrix of the pie and pre-thickening that liquid prior to baking, you will get the perfect ratio of apple to "apple goo" in every bite and a perfect apple pie every time!

BANANA BLUEBERRY
Crunch

MAKES ONE 9-INCH PIE

WHAT YOU NEED
- Pie dough for a Standard Single Crust (page 35)
- 9-inch standard pie plate
- Immersion circulator with water bath
- Vacuum sealer
- Pie crust shield or foil (see page 19)

In this recipe, perfectly cooked blueberries are suspended in a matrix of roasted banana—an unexpected yet delicious combination. In addition to flavor, the bananas also provide structure, allowing for neat and tidy slices of pie. This pie is topped with an addictive buttery bananagraham topping, giving a satisfying crunch to the fruity filling.

1. START THE FILLING: Spread the blueberries on a half sheet pan (make sure they're in a single layer so they freeze individually rather than in one large clump) and put them in the freezer until frozen (at least a couple of hours). If you have a small freezer that cannot accommodate a large pan, just dry the berries really well and freeze them in a smaller container.

2. When the blueberries are almost frozen, set up the water bath for your immersion circulator and start heating the water to 150°F (see the sous vide instructions on page 28).

recipe continues

INGREDIENT	VOLUME	WEIGHT (STANDARD)	WEIGHT (METRIC)
FILLING			
Blueberries	5 cups	30 ounces	850 grams
Finely ground quick-cooking tapioca, such as Minute	2 tablespoons	0.7 ounce	20 grams
Turbinado sugar	¾ cup	5.25 ounces	150 grams
Salt	⅛ teaspoon		
Ground cinnamon	⅛ teaspoon		
Ground nutmeg	⅛ teaspoon		
Ground cloves	⅛ teaspoon		
Unsalted butter	1 tablespoon	0.5 ounce	14 grams
Bananas, peeled and sliced (weighed after peeling)	4 medium	14 ounces	400 grams
BANANAGRAHAM TOPPING			
Freeze-dried bananas	¾ cup	1.2 ounces	34 grams
Turbinado sugar	¼ cup	1.75 ounces	50 grams
Salt	pinch		
Ground cinnamon	⅛ teaspoon		
Graham crackers	6 sheets	3.4 ounces	96 grams
Unsalted butter, melted	4 tablespoons	2 ounces	57 grams

3. PARTIALLY BLIND-BAKE THE CRUST: Follow the instructions on page 47. The pie will bake longer after the filling is added, so it should not be completely browned at this point. Remove the pie dish from the oven, set it on a wire cooling rack, and remove the foil or parchment and pie weights. Keep the oven at 350°F.

4. CONTINUE MAKING THE FILLING: Transfer the frozen blueberries to a vacuum sealable bag. Add the tapioca, ½ cup/3.5 ounces/100 grams of the turbinado sugar, the salt, cinnamon, nutmeg, and cloves. Gently shake the bag to disperse the contents, vacuum-seal the bag, and then sous vide the blueberries in the water bath for 1 hour.

5. While the blueberries are in the water bath, melt the butter in a nonstick skillet along with the remaining ¼ cup/1.75 ounces/50 grams of turbinado sugar. Add the bananas, cover the pan, and turn the heat to low for 10 minutes.

6. Uncover the pan. The bananas should have softened and look like they are sitting in a pool of liquid. If they have not, turn up the heat, cover the pan, and check the bananas every 2 minutes until they have softened. Increase the heat to medium-high to bring the banana liquid to a boil. Keep stirring with a rubber spatula, pressing on the bananas until they soften into a paste and the liquid has completely evaporated, about 5 minutes. The bananas will start to caramelize and concentrate. Keep breaking up and flipping the banana paste until fully caramelized and concentrated, about another 10 to 15 minutes, then remove it from the heat. You should have approximately 1½ cups/7.6 to 8.8 ounces/215 to 250 grams of caramelized banana paste. Transfer the paste to a large mixing bowl and set it aside.

7. MAKE THE BANANAGRAHAM TOPPING: In a food processor, pulse the freeze-dried bananas several times until mostly ground. Add the turbinado sugar, salt, and cinnamon and continue to pulse until the mixture is finely ground. Transfer to a small bowl and, using your fingers, break the graham crackers directly into the bowl until almost crumbs. The goal is to retain some ¼-inch pieces along with the smaller crumbs. Add the melted butter and stir, using either your fingers or a rubber spatula, forming a crumbly bananagraham topping. Set aside.

8. Remove the bag with the blueberry mixture from the water bath and place it on a kitchen towel to cool for 5 minutes. Cut a ¼-inch opening in a corner of the bag and pour the blueberry juice into the bowl with the banana paste, reserving the berries in the bag for now. Whisk the banana paste until well mixed with the juice. Open the bag fully and pour the remaining contents into the bowl. Place the bag flat on the countertop and use a bench scraper to squeeze any remaining blueberry mixture toward the bag opening and into the bowl. Gently fold the berries into the loosened banana paste.

BLUEBERRY BLUES

When we moved to our house, there was a large backyard that was mostly unused by the previous owners. In addition to agricultural endeavors discussed elsewhere in this book, we thought it would be a great idea to plant blueberry bushes along the fence so we could have our own farm-fresh supply of blueberries every year. The birds and squirrels also thought it was a great idea. We became their new best friends. As it turns out, we're able to harvest a good *handful* of berries every year, once the neighborhood wildlife have had their fill. That's right, a whole handful! Now we just need to develop a recipe that yields a single blueberry muffin and it will have all been worthwhile. Fortunately, Georgia is filled with actual blueberry farmers providing us with an ample supply of fruit. We stock up in the summertime, vacuum-seal, and freeze the blueberries (along with many other seasonal fruits) for use throughout the year.

9. FILL THE CRUST AND BAKE: Pour the mixture into the warm pie shell. Press down on the filling using the rubber spatula or a small offset spatula, creating a flat surface for the topping. Sprinkle the bananagraham topping in an even layer across the surface of the pie. Cover the edges of the pie with a pie crust shield and bake on the bottom rack of the oven for 20 minutes or until the topping is just starting to toast slightly.

10. Remove the pie from the oven, place on a cooling rack, and allow the pie to cool completely, at least 4 hours, before serving. (Leftovers can be stored, covered, at room temperature for up to 3 days.)

Tahitian
PINEAPPLE

MAKES ONE 9½-INCH DEEP-DISH PIE

WHAT YOU NEED
- Pie dough for a Deep-Dish Single Crust (page 36)
- 9½-inch deep-dish pie plate
- Pie crust shield or foil (see page 19)
- 3 piping bags (see page 21) fitted with Ateco or Wilton #2 round tips, or 3 plastic squeeze bottles with medium nozzles

You know that luscious vanilla-scented brown sugar topping that surrounds the caramelized rings of fruit on a pineapple upside-down cake? *That!* We needed more of that in our lives, so we developed this pie packed with fresh pineapple cooked in browned butter and paired with floral vanilla and caramel notes of turbinado sugar. The vanilla-sweetened panko topping adds a satisfying crunch to every bite. The pie can be completed with a simple drizzle of glaze on top, or see the Blue Ribbon Bonus on page 121 to create a perfectly piped pineapple using royal icing.

1. PARTIALLY BLIND-BAKE THE CRUST: Follow the instructions on page 47. The pie will bake longer after the filling is added, so it should not be completely browned at this point. Remove the pie dish from the oven, set it on a wire cooling rack, and remove the foil or parchment and pie weights. Keep the oven at 350°F and adjust the oven rack to the lowest position.

2. MAKE THE CRUNCHY TOPPING: Melt the butter in a small bowl. Using a small rubber spatula, stir in the vanilla, sugar, and salt (the sugar will remain mostly undissolved; that is okay). Add the panko and stir until all the crumbs are coated with the sugar mixture; set aside.

recipe continues

INGREDIENT	VOLUME	WEIGHT (STANDARD)	WEIGHT (METRIC)
CRUNCHY TOPPING			
Unsalted butter	5 tablespoons	2.5 ounces	71 grams
Vanilla extract	1 teaspoon		
Turbinado sugar	⅓ cup	2.35 ounces	67 grams
Salt	pinch		
Panko breadcrumbs (unseasoned)	1¼ cups	2.5 ounces	71 grams
PINEAPPLE FILLING			
Unsalted butter	4 tablespoons	2 ounces	57 grams
Fresh pineapples, about 2 medium, cut into ½- to 1-inch chunks	5 cups	34 ounces	964 grams
Finely grated lime zest	1 teaspoon		
Granny Smith apple	1 medium	about 6.5 ounces	about 184 grams
Fresh lime juice	2 tablespoons	1 ounce	28 grams
Turbinado sugar	1 cup	7 ounces	200 grams
Finely ground quick-cooking tapioca, such as Minute	2 tablespoons plus 2 teaspons	1 ounce	28 grams
Salt	⅛ teaspoon		
Vanilla extract	2 teaspoons		

INGREDIENT	VOLUME	WEIGHT (STANDARD)	WEIGHT (METRIC)
GLAZE (OPTIONAL)			
Confectioners' sugar	1½ cups	6 ounces	170 grams
Heavy cream	2 tablespoons	1 ounce	29 grams
Pineapple juice	2 tablespoons	1 ounce	28 grams
Vanilla extract	¼ teaspoon		
Salt	pinch		
Gel food colors (gold, egg yellow, leaf green, and forest green) (optional)	1 drop each		

3. MAKE THE PINEAPPLE FILLING: Melt the butter in a large saucepan over medium-high heat and continue cooking until it starts to brown. Swirl the pan and keep a close eye on it to make sure it is not getting too dark; you are aiming for a medium-brown shade that smells nutty (not black and burnt). Immediately stir in the pineapple chunks and lime zest with a rubber spatula. The pineapple will start to release some liquid. Allow that liquid to boil, then reduce the heat to low so that the liquid is just simmering. Cover the pan for 5 minutes.

4. Meanwhile, peel the apple and grate it using the coarse holes of a box grater. Wrap the grated apple in a clean, lint-free kitchen towel and squeeze to remove as much of the juice as possible (it's best to do this over a sink; you don't need to save the squeezed juice). Add the grated apple and lime juice to the pineapple, stirring to combine.

5. In a small bowl, mix the sugar, ground tapioca, and salt together. Pour this mixture into the saucepan and return to medium-high heat, stirring with the rubber spatula until the sugar is dissolved and the liquid starts to bubble. Turn off the heat and add the vanilla.

6. FILL THE CRUST AND BAKE: Pour the mixture into the warm pie shell. Press down on the filling using the rubber spatula or a small offset spatula, creating a flat surface for the topping. Using your fingers, sprinkle the panko topping in an even layer across the surface of the pie. Cover the edges of the pie with a pie crust shield (or a foil shield, page 19) and bake on the bottom rack of the oven until the topping is evenly golden brown, about 24 minutes, rotating the pie every 8 minutes to ensure even browning.

7. Remove the pie from the oven, place on a cooling rack, and allow the pie to cool completely before glazing, at least 4 hours.

8. MAKE THE OPTIONAL DECORATIVE GLAZE: Measure the confectioners' sugar directly into a medium bowl. Add the cream, pineapple juice, vanilla, and salt and stir with a small whisk until smooth. Lift the whisk and watch the glaze fall to assess the consistency. It should flow smoothly like corn syrup or thick shampoo. If too thick, stir in a bit more cream or pineapple juice by the teaspoonful until the glaze has reached a smooth flowing consistency. If the mixture is too thin, stir in additional teaspoons of confectioners' sugar until the right consistency is reached.

9. Divide this glaze into thirds by pouring portions (3 to 4 tablespoons) into two smaller bowls. Add the yellow food colorings to one and the greens to the other, leaving the third one white. Pour all three glazes into squeeze bottles with medium nozzles or into piping bags fitted with #2 piping tips.

10. The surface of the pie is now your blank canvas. Draw a pineapple! It is actually simpler than you think. Starting with the yellow glaze, draw the outline of the body of the pineapple; an oval. Fill in the pineapple by drawing a series of diagonal lines like an argyle sock pattern. Switch now to the green glaze to draw the crown on top of the pineapple. This is simply a series of arcing zigzag lines atop the pineapple body. Once outlined, fill in the leaves with additional green glaze. Use the white glaze for some artistic flourishes around the pineapple, ensuring that each slice of pie will be accented by some of the glaze.

11. Serve the pie when cooled to room temperature and glaze has set. (Leftovers can be stored, covered, at room temperature for up to 3 days.)

BLUE RIBBON BONUS:

A Perfectly Piped Pineapple

Instead of using the glaze to decorate the top of this pie, a batch of royal icing can be used to create a perfectly piped pineapple instead. Divide one batch of piping-consistency royal icing (page 259) in half and color one half yellow and the other half green. Add the yellow icing to the piping bag fitted with a Wilton #17 star piping tip. Add the green icing to the piping bag fitted with a Wilton #352 leaf piping tip. Pipe stars of the yellow icing in the barrel-like shape of a pineapple over about two-thirds the diameter of the pie. With the sharp points of the piping tip positioned up and down, use the green icing to pipe the leaves at the top of the pineapple shape.

WEST INDIES

Wedding

If you grew up in the Caribbean, as Paul did, you can't host a wedding without offering black cake. To make it, you soak dried fruits, almonds, and exotic spices in a healthy dose of liquor, sometimes for months, before baking the mixture in a dark, richly flavored fruitcake batter. This months-long preparation elevates the black cake to cult status, and people lose their minds when gifted with just a few bites. Newly engaged couples know that their first order of business after popping the question is to find a black cake baker (many of whom have their own secret recipe). Paul used his grandmother's recipe to create mini black cakes for our wedding, and they are what inspired this West Indies Wedding pie. If you don't want to include the alcohol (most of it burns off in the oven, leaving just the flavor behind), substitute ¼ cup of apple cider for the brandies and cherry liqueur.

MAKES ONE 9-INCH PIE

WHAT YOU NEED
- Pie dough for Standard Single Crust (page 35)
- 9-inch standard pie plate
- Pie crust shield or foil (see page 19)
- Molasses Whipped Cream (page 258), for serving

1. PARTIALLY BLIND-BAKE THE CRUST: Follow the instructions on page 47. The pie will bake longer after the filling is added, so it should not be completely browned at this point. Remove the pie dish from the oven, set it on a wire cooling rack, and remove the foil or parchment and pie weights. Keep the oven at 350°F.

2. MAKE THE STREUSEL TOPPING: Line a 13 by 9-inch pan with parchment or wax paper. Pulse the almonds, flour, muscovado sugar, cinnamon, and salt in the bowl of a food processor until finely chopped. Pour in the melted butter and pulse until the flour is moistened. Add the oats and pulse a few more times to chop and incorporate the oats. Pour the mixture into the prepared pan, breaking apart any large clumps and pinching together some of the smaller bits into ¼- to ½-inch nuggets. Place the pan in the freezer until ready to use (cover the pan with foil if you plan on storing the unbaked nuggets for more than a few hours; they keep in the freezer for a few days).

recipe continues

INGREDIENT	VOLUME	WEIGHT (STANDARD)	WEIGHT (METRIC)
STREUSEL TOPPING (can be prepared a few days in advance)			
Slivered almonds	½ cup	2.1 ounces	60 grams
All-purpose flour	½ cup	2.5 ounces	71 grams
Dark muscovado sugar, lightly packed (see page 124)	¼ cup	1.75 ounces	50 grams
Ground cinnamon	¼ teaspoon		
Salt	⅛ teaspoon		
Unsalted butter, melted	6 tablespoons	3 ounces	85 grams
Old-fashioned rolled oats	½ cup	1.75 ounces	50 grams

INGREDIENT	VOLUME	WEIGHT (STANDARD)	WEIGHT (METRIC)
FILLING			
Dark raisins	1⅔ cups	8 ounces	227 grams
Pitted prunes, quartered	¾ cup	4 ounces	113 grams
Dried currants	¾ cup	4 ounces	113 grams
Dark muscovado sugar (see below right)	¼ cup	1.75 ounces	50 grams
Ground cinnamon	¾ teaspoon		
Ground nutmeg	¼ teaspoon		
Ground allspice	¼ teaspoon		
Salt	½ teaspoon		
Brandy	2 tablespoons	1 ounce	28 grams
Cherry liqueur, such as Heering	2 tablespoons	1.15 ounces	33 grams
Blackberry brandy	2 tablespoons	1 ounce	28 grams
Heavy cream	⅔ cup	5.45 ounces	155 grams
Whole milk	⅔ cup	5.65 ounces	161 grams
Eggs	4 large		

3. MAKE THE FILLING: Add the raisins, prunes, currants, muscovado sugar, cinnamon, nutmeg, allspice, salt, brandy, cherry liqueur, and blackberry brandy to a small saucepan and bring to a simmer over medium-high heat. When the mixture begins to simmer, turn off the heat, cover, and let the fruits steam for 10 minutes.

4. Transfer the fruit mixture to the bowl of a food processor and process until finely pureed. Pour in the cream and milk through the feed tube and continue processing until just combined. Add the eggs, one at a time, pulsing for three 1-second pulses between each.

5. FILL THE CRUST AND BAKE: Pour the mixture into the warm pie shell and bake on the middle oven rack until the top is firmed up just enough so the topping doesn't sink down—this takes 10 minutes.

6. Remove the pie from the oven and evenly sprinkle the frozen topping nuggets on top. Cover the crust edge with a pie shield and bake until the topping is slightly browned and the filling is set and no longer shakes when jostled, 25 to 30 more minutes.

7. Remove the pie from the oven, place on a cooling rack, and allow the pie to cool to room temperature, about 4 hours, before refrigerating to chill completely, about 4 more hours or overnight. (Leftovers can be stored in the refrigerator for up to 2 days.) Serve the pie with dollops of Molasses Whipped Cream for the full experience.

THE GUYS TALK PIES

Muscovado is a very dark brown sugar that tastes of molasses or dark rum—flavor elements that are present in traditional West Indies black cake. We encourage you to seek it out and use it for this pie (see Sources, page 265). If you have difficulty finding it, substitute a similar weight of dark brown sugar (even though Chris would say that's a quitter's attitude!).

RHUBARB-GOOSEBERRY

MAKES ONE 9-INCH PIE

WHAT YOU NEED

- Pie dough for a Standard Double Crust (page 35)
- 9-inch standard pie plate
- Immersion circulator with water bath
- Vacuum sealer
- Pie crust shield or foil (see page 19)
- ½-inch- to 1-inch-long cookie or fondant cutters (see Sources, page 265)

Rhubarb is a vegetable that, when sold at market, looks like large mutant stalks of red celery, making it especially hard to believe that it is actually completely unrelated to and tastes nothing like celery. Gooseberries are small round fruits, less than one inch in size, that look like lightly veined marbles either red or green in color, depending on the variety. If you haven't had either of these before, you should definitely make this pie to experience some wonderful new flavors. With just enough sugar to balance their tartness, they blend well and complement each other for a delicate treat. This pie presents a wonderful opportunity to go exploring in the produce section of your grocery store or get to know a farmer in your greenmarket to see when the rhubarb and gooseberries are coming to market.

1. If using pre-chopped frozen rhubarb and frozen gooseberries, start at Step 2. To prepare the filling, chop the fresh rhubarb into ½-inch dice and place it on a half sheet pan. Place the pan in the freezer until frozen (at least a couple of hours). Spread the gooseberries on a half sheet pan and put them in the freezer until frozen (at least 2 hours). Spread them out as much as possible to allow them to freeze individually rather than in one large clump.

2. Set up the water bath for your immersion circulator and start heating the water to 150°F (see sous vide instructions, page 28).

3. Transfer the frozen gooseberries and rhubarb to a vacuum-sealable bag. Squeeze the grated apple (using a clean tea towel works well) to remove as much of the juice as possible and disperse the grated apple inside the bag. (You don't need to save the squeezed juice.) Add the tapioca, sugar, salt, and ginger. Gently shake the bag to disperse the contents and then vacuum-seal it shut.

4. Cook the gooseberry mixture sous vide in the water bath for 1 hour, flipping the bag halfway through to ensure that the contents are well mixed.

recipe continues

INGREDIENT	VOLUME	WEIGHT (STANDARD)	WEIGHT (METRIC)
Rhubarb, fresh or frozen and trimmed	2 medium stalks	10 ounces	283 grams
Gooseberries, fresh or frozen	4 cups	21 ounces	600 grams
Granny Smith apple, peeled and grated	1 medium	6.5 ounces	184 grams
Finely ground quick-cooking tapioca, such as Minute	2 tablespoons plus 1 teaspoon	0.85 ounce	24 grams
Sugar	1½ cups	10.5 ounces	300 grams
Salt	⅛ teaspoon		
Ground ginger	¼ teaspoon		
Egg yolk	1 large		
Heavy cream	1 tablespoon	0.5 ounce	15 grams

5. While the gooseberry mixture is cooking, prepare the crust. Roll out the largest disc of dough to a ⅛-inch thickness (see page 42), and place in a 9-inch pie pan. Place the pie pan with the untrimmed pie dough in the refrigerator.

6. Roll out the second disc of dough into an approximately 12-inch, ⅛-inch-thick circle. If you have rolled it on a silicone mat, transfer the dough to a piece of parchment (do not attempt to cut your dough on the silicone mat; you may end up cutting right through the silicone as well as the pie dough). Use ½-inch- to 1-inch-long cookie or fondant cutters of any shape to cut out small pieces of dough to create a cutout top crust. Start in the center of the dough and work your way outward, creating a symmetrical pattern of shapes. Leave at least ¼ inch of dough between the cutout shapes. Your final pattern should be just under 9 inches in diameter to cover the surface of the pie but should not extend over the rim of the pie plate. Slide the parchment paper and cutout top crust onto the back of a baking sheet and place it in the freezer until you are ready to assemble the pie.

7. Remove the bag of gooseberries from the water bath and place it on a kitchen towel to cool for 5 minutes. Cut open the bag and pour the contents into the untrimmed pie shell that has been chilling in the refrigerator. Use a bench scraper to get out any residual contents; at this point the berries will still appear intact and the rhubarb will have softened considerably, releasing a beautiful pink liquid.

8. Place the prepared cutout top crust from the freezer on top of the pie. The heat from the gooseberry mixture, along with the warmth from your fingers, will start to soften the crust. Press the bottom and top edges of the crusts together, rotating the pie as you go. Keep rotating and pressing until the top and bottom is sealed. Trim the excess and roll the edge under, crimp it decoratively (see page 24), and place the pie in the freezer for 20 minutes. Adjust an oven rack to the lowest position and heat the oven to 425°F.

9. Stir the yolk and cream together to make an egg wash. Brush the top of the pie with the egg wash.

10. Place the pie on the bottom oven rack and immediately reduce the temperature to 400°F. After 15 minutes, rotate the pie and add a pie crust shield to protect the edges. Bake an additional 40 minutes, or until the liquid just barely starts to bubble at the edges, rotating halfway through.

11. Remove the pie from the oven, place on a cooling rack, and allow it to cool to room temperature before slicing. (Leftovers can be stored, covered, at room temperature for up to 3 days.)

Chocolate-Covered
CHERRY

MAKES ONE 9½-INCH DEEP-DISH PIE

WHAT YOU NEED

- Pie dough for a Cocoa Pastry Crust (page 40)
- 9½-inch deep-dish pie plate
- 8½-inch tart ring
- Immersion circulator and water bath
- Vacuum sealer
- Cherry cookie cutter (see Sources, page 265)
- Pie crust shield or foil (see page 19)

In this pie, the tender sour cherries are reinforced with the addition of chewier dried cherries. Chopped sweet cherries are added to the mix to help thicken the pie and add even more layers of cherry flavor. All this cherry goodness is then encased in chocolate, taking it to a whole new level. The topping for this pie needs to be prepared at least 4 hours (or up to 2 weeks) in advance to allow it to freeze. Once frozen, the topping can be unmolded, wrapped in plastic, and stored in the freezer until you are ready to make the pie.

1. MAKE THE CHOCOLATE TOPPING: Place the graham crackers, almond paste, butter, egg, golden syrup, and melted chocolate into the bowl of a food processor. Process until fully mixed, about 1 minute.

2. Place an 8½-inch tart ring on a baking sheet lined with a silicone mat. Alternatively, draw an 8½-inch circle on a piece of parchment and flip it over on the baking sheet (so you can still see the circle but won't get ink on your food). Using an offset spatula, spread the chocolate graham paste evenly inside the mold/circle, getting it as smooth and level as you can. Place the pan in the freezer for at least 4 hours, until frozen solid.

recipe continues

INGREDIENT	VOLUME	WEIGHT (STANDARD)	WEIGHT (METRIC)
CHOCOLATE TOPPING (prepare 4 hours–2 weeks ahead)			
Graham crackers	7 sheets	4 ounces	113 grams
Almond paste	3 tablespoons	1.5 ounces	42 grams
Unsalted butter, at room temperature	4 tablespoons	2 ounces	57 grams
Egg	1 large		
Golden syrup (or light corn syrup)	1 tablespoon		
Bittersweet chocolate, melted		3 ounces	85 grams
FILLING			
Finely ground quick-cooking tapioca, such as Minute	2½ tablespoons	0.9 ounce	25 grams
Sugar	1 scant cup	6.7 ounces	190 grams
Salt	⅛ teaspoon		
Frozen sweet cherries	¾ cup	3 ounces	85 grams
Fresh lemon juice	1 tablespoon	0.5 ounce	14 grams
Almond extract	¼ teaspoon		
Frozen sour cherries	3½ cups	21 ounces	600 grams
Dried sour cherries	⅔ cup	3 ounces	85 grams

3. **MAKE THE FILLING:** Set up the water bath for your immersion circulator and start heating the water to 150°F (see sous vide instructions on page 28). Place the tapioca, sugar, and salt into a vacuum-sealable bag and shake it around until ingredients are well mixed. Roughly chop the frozen sweet cherries into ¼-inch dice and add them to the bag with the sugar. Add the lemon juice, almond extract, frozen sour cherries, and dried sour cherries. Gently shake the bag to disperse the contents and then vacuum-seal it shut. Cook the cherries sous vide in the water bath for 1 hour.

4. **PARTIALLY BLIND-BAKE THE CRUST:** Follow the instructions on page 47. The pie will bake longer after the filling is added, so it should not be completely baked at this point. Remove the pie dish from the oven, set it on a wire cooling rack, and remove the foil or parchment and pie weights. Keep the oven at 350°F.

5. Reroll the crust trimmings to a ⅛-inch thickness (see page 42) and cut out a decorative shape using a cherry-shaped cookie cutter. Place the cherry cutout in the freezer along with the topping disc.

6. **FILL THE CRUST AND BAKE:** Remove the cherry bag from the water bath and dry it off with a kitchen towel. Place a pie crust shield on the pie to prevent splashes. Cut open the bag and pour the filling into the warm crust. Use a bench scraper to squeegee out any residual contents. The filling will look quite loose at this point (don't worry—it will thicken up).

7. Remove the frozen chocolate topping disc from the freezer. Peel off the silicone mat/parchment. To unmold the disc, gently press around the edge of the disc with your thumbs. The disc will loosen and then fall away from the mold. Place the frozen disc of chocolate topping smooth side up on top of the filled pie. If it is a tight fit, gently press it down so that it is sitting on the surface of the cherries and abutting the crust edge. Place the decorative cherry shape in the center of the chocolate disc. Cover the edges of the pie with a pie crust shield and bake on the middle rack of the oven for 35 minutes. The topping will have puffed slightly and set.

8. Remove the pie from the oven, place on a cooling rack, and allow the pie to cool completely, at least 4 hours, before serving. (Leftovers can be stored, covered, at room temperature for up to 3 days.)

FINDING (AND LOSING) OUR CHERRIES

Paul has a bit of an obsession with sour cherries. One Saturday morning, we actually found fresh sour cherries at the market, just sitting there like a rare Pokémon. (What is a Pokémon? We're not sure, but we figure we'd sound slightly cool if we mentioned it.) We captured them and headed home with a new purpose for that afternoon. That cherry pie was amazing; we had to have more. But there were no sour cherries to be had. Every summer, we'd set out to scour the fresh produce sections around the city, with no luck. So, we decided to try to grow our own! We ordered two sour cherry trees from an online nursery. When the box arrived with our saplings, we excitedly planted them and waited. After a couple years of careful tending they had grown into respectable-looking trees. One spring, they started to flower. We saw bees buzzing around the trees doing their thing. Yes—everything was coming along! We began to dream of all the wonderful pie creations we would make with our own private cherry harvest. The flower petals fell, and we noticed teeny tiny fruits starting to swell at the bases. How exciting! They continued to grow, and grow, and grow some more. When they reached golf ball size, it became apparent that we were successfully growing something—but not cherries. Turns out, we can't tell the difference between a cherry tree and an apple tree (and neither could that nursery that has since gone out of business). Thank goodness in the meantime we finally found a source for frozen sour cherries (see page 265) to sate our summer craving.

Italian Plum
AFFOGATO

MAKES ONE 9½-INCH DEEP-DISH PIE

WHAT YOU NEED
- Pie dough for a Deep-Dish Single Crust (page 36)
- 9½-inch deep-dish pie plate
- Immersion circulator with water bath
- Vacuum sealer
- Pie crust shield or foil (see page 19)
- Piping bag (see page 21) fitted with a Wilton #4B or other large star piping tip

Alice Medrich has a recipe for Italian prune plums poached in coffee and brandy served over vanilla ice cream. After stumbling across these plums in our farmers' market, we tried her recipe and decided that this delicious concoction had to be converted into a pie. Thanks Alice! We're happy to note that these plums have returned to our market every summer. If you can't find these particular plums, the recipe also works with fresh apricots or thawed frozen sweet cherries.

1. START THE MASCARPONE TOPPING: In a medium microwave-safe bowl, microwave the cream until it just starts to boil, 1 to 2 minutes, depending on the power of your microwave oven. Using a rubber spatula, stir in the sugar, espresso powder, and vanilla until the sugar and espresso are dissolved. Cover the bowl with plastic wrap and place it in the refrigerator until cold, at least 2 hours.

2. MAKE THE FILLING: Set up the water bath for your immersion circulator and start heating the water to 150°F (see sous vide instructions on page 28). Peel the apple and grate it using the coarse holes of a box grater. Discard the peels and core. Squeeze the grated apple to remove as much of the juice as possible and break up the clump of grated apple inside a large vacuum-sealable bag. Add the sliced plums, vanilla, and brandy to the bag.

recipe continues

INGREDIENT	VOLUME	WEIGHT (STANDARD)	WEIGHT (METRIC)
MASCARPONE TOPPING			
Heavy cream	¾ cup	6.15 ounces	174 grams
Sugar	⅔ cup	4.65 ounces	133 grams
Instant espresso powder	2 teaspoons		
Vanilla extract	1 teaspoon		
Mascarpone cheese, cold	1 cup	8 ounces	227 grams
FILLING			
Granny Smith apple	1 medium	about 6.5 ounces	about 184 grams
Italian prune plums, pitted and sliced (from approximately 2 pounds whole)	5 cups	30 ounces	850 grams
Vanilla extract	1 teaspoon		
Brandy	2 tablespoons	1 ounce	28 grams
Finely ground quick-cooking tapioca, such as Minute	2 tablespoons plus 2 teaspoons	1 ounce	28 grams
Sugar	1 cup	7 ounces	200 grams
Instant espresso powder	2 tablespoons	0.25 ounce	7 grams
Salt	⅛ teaspoon		

3. In a small bowl, whisk the tapioca, sugar, espresso powder, and salt until well mixed. Pour this mixture into the vacuum bag, and vacuum-seal it shut. Cook the plums sous vide in the water bath for 1 hour.

4. PARTIALLY BLIND-BAKE THE CRUST: Follow the instructions on page 47. The pie will bake longer after the filling is added, so it should not be completely browned at this point. Remove the pie dish from the oven, set it on a wire cooling rack, and remove the foil or parchment and pie weights. Keep the oven at 350°F.

5. FILL THE CRUST AND BAKE: Remove the plum bag from the water bath, and dry it off with a kitchen towel. Place a pie crust shield on the pie to prevent splashes. Cut open the bag and pour the filling into the warm crust. Use a bench scraper to get out all the juices. The filling will look quite loose at this point, but don't worry; it will thicken up in the oven.

6. Keep the pie crust shield on and bake on the bottom rack of the oven until the plum filling starts to gently bubble at the edges, about 25 minutes.

7. Remove the pie from the oven, remove the pie crust shield, place the pie on a cooling rack, and allow the pie to cool completely, at least 4 hours, before serving.

8. ADD THE TOPPING: When ready to serve the pie, complete the filling by adding the mascarpone cheese to the chilled espresso cream. Beat with an electric mixer until stiff peaks form, about 2 minutes. Spread this topping onto the chilled pie and smooth with an offset spatula or pipe it decoratively on top of the pie using the prepared bag. (Any leftovers can be stored in the refrigerator for up to 3 days.)

STICKY TOFFEE

Pudding

WHAT YOU NEED
- Pie dough for a Deep-Dish Single Crust (page 36)
- 9½-inch deep-dish pie plate
- Pie crust shield or foil (see page 19)
- Instant-read thermometer

Have you noticed how many pies in this book advise you to wait until the pie has at least cooled to room temperature before eating it? It's as if we think you are all masters of self-control who are not desperately in need of pie *right now*. Fear not! This is a pie designed to eat when it is still warm from the oven. Made with dates, butter, and brown sugar, the pie has an almost cakelike consistency. Right after baking, the hot pie is slathered with a warm toffee sauce that soaks right into the filling and makes it irresistible.

1. PARTIALLY BLIND-BAKE THE CRUST: Follow the instructions on page 47. The pie will bake longer after the filling is added, so it should not be completely browned at this point. Remove the pie dish from the oven, set it on a wire cooling rack, and remove the foil or parchment and pie weights. Decrease the oven temperature to 275°F.

2. MAKE THE FILLING: When the crust is almost finished baking, start the filling. Put the chopped dates in a medium saucepan with 1 cup/ 8.35 ounces/236 grams water. Bring the dates to a boil and turn off the heat. Stir in the baking soda with a rubber spatula. The dates will start to foam and then mostly fall apart.

recipe continues

INGREDIENT	VOLUME	WEIGHT (STANDARD)	WEIGHT (METRIC)
FILLING			
Dried dates, pitted and chopped	1⅓ cups	8 ounces	227 grams
Baking soda	1 teaspoon		
Unsalted butter, melted	4 tablespoons	2 ounces	57 grams
Dark brown sugar, lightly packed	¾ cup	5.25 ounces	150 grams
Cane syrup, such as Steen's (see Sources, page 265)	2 tablespoons	1.5 ounces	43 grams
Eggs	2 large		
Vanilla extract	1 teaspoon		
All-purpose flour	1 cup	5 ounces	142 grams
Baking powder	¾ teaspoon		
Salt	½ teaspoon		
TOFFEE SAUCE			
Heavy cream	½ cup	4.1 ounces	116 grams
Unsalted butter	4 tablespoons	2 ounces	57 grams
Dark brown sugar, lightly packed	¼ cup	1.75 ounces	50 grams
Cane syrup, such as Steen's (see Sources, page 265)	1 tablespoon	0.75 ounce	21 grams
Salt	⅛ teaspoon		
Vanilla extract	1 teaspoon		

3. In a medium microwave-safe bowl, whisk together the melted butter, brown sugar, and cane syrup, then whisk in the eggs and vanilla. Fold in the flour, baking powder, and salt until well mixed. Stir in the date mixture. When fully incorporated, check the temperature of the batter. If it is less than 125°F, microwave the mixture, checking the temperature and stirring every 30 seconds, until it reaches 125°F.

4. **FILL THE CRUST AND BAKE:** Place a pie crust shield on the pie and pour the filling into the warm crust. Bake until the filling has puffed considerably and is set, about 1 hour. If still jiggly in the middle, keep baking, checking every 5 minutes until it has set. When you remove the pie from the oven, immediately poke the surface all over with a toothpick or small skewer (about 30 pokes). Poke deep into the filling but do not poke through the crust on the bottom.

5. **MAKE THE TOFFEE SAUCE:** Pour the cream into a small saucepan over medium heat and bring it to a boil, stirring with a rubber spatula until it has thickened and reduced in volume by about one-third, 5 to 10 minutes. Add the butter, brown sugar, cane syrup, and salt and bring it back to a boil, stirring until the butter has melted, the sugar has dissolved, and the mixture is uniform. Turn off the heat and stir in the vanilla.

6. Pour about one-third of the warm toffee sauce onto the still-warm pie. Using a small offset spatula, keep spreading the sauce over the surface of the hot pie. As you spread, it will soak into the filling. Repeat this process with the remainder of the sauce. This pie is best when served still warm from the oven, so don't wait too long before going for it. The warm pie pairs well with a small scoop of vanilla ice cream, but it pairs even better with a large scoop of vanilla ice cream. (Refrigerate leftovers for up to 3 days; we like to warm slices in the microwave before serving.)

Purple
PLUM

MAKES ONE 9½-INCH DEEP-DISH PIE

WHAT YOU NEED
- Pie dough for a Deep-Dish Single Crust (page 36)
- 9½-inch deep-dish pie plate
- 8½-inch tart ring
- Pie crust shield or foil (see page 19)

Italian prune plums are a purple-skinned, elongated, almost egg-shaped fruit with pale flesh that is denser than your average plum. The fresh fruits are quite tart and so are ideal for pie. In this one, the plums are frozen and thawed, which accomplishes two things: it softens the fruits and it releases juice from the plums. That plum juice is combined with pureed blueberries for an explosion of purple fruit flavor. If you can't find the plums in your market, apricots are a reasonable (but not actually purple) substitute.

1. MAKE THE GRAHAM-BLUEBERRY TOPPING: Process the freeze-dried blueberries in the bowl of a food processor until finely ground, about 30 seconds. Add the graham crackers, butter, egg, corn syrup, and melted white chocolate. Process until a thick paste forms. Place an 8½-inch tart ring on a baking sheet lined with a silicone mat. Alternatively, draw an 8½-inch circle on a piece of parchment and flip it over on the baking sheet (so you can still see the circle but won't get ink on your food). Using an offset spatula, spread the blueberry graham paste evenly inside the mold/circle, getting it as smooth and level as you can. Place the pan in the freezer for at least 4 hours, until frozen solid. Or prepare the topping up to 2 weeks in advance. Once frozen, it can be unmolded, wrapped in plastic wrap, and stored in the freezer until you are ready to make the pie.

recipe continues

INGREDIENT	VOLUME	WEIGHT (STANDARD)	WEIGHT (METRIC)
GRAHAM-BLUEBERRY TOPPING (can be made and frozen up to 2 weeks ahead)			
Freeze-dried blueberries	1 cup	1 ounce	28 grams
Graham crackers	7 sheets	4 ounces	113 grams
Unsalted butter, softened	5 tablespoons	2.5 ounces	71 grams
Egg	1 large		
Light corn syrup	1 tablespoon		
White chocolate, melted		3 ounces	85 grams
PURPLE PLUM FILING			
Italian prune plums, pitted, sliced, and frozen (from approximately 2½ pounds whole)	5½ cups	34 ounces	964 grams
Blueberries	2 cups	10 ounces	283 grams
Vanilla extract	2 teaspoons		
Fresh lemon juice	1 teaspoon		
Tapioca starch	2 tablespoons	0.5 ounce	15 grams
Cornstarch	2 tablespoons	0.55 ounce	15 grams
Sugar	1 cup	7 ounces	200 grams
Salt	⅛ teaspoon		
Ground cinnamon	¼ teaspoon		

INGREDIENT	VOLUME
DECORATION	
Purple Royal Icing (page 259), at a honey consistency	1 recipe

2. PARTIALLY BLIND-BAKE THE CRUST: Follow the instructions on page 47. The pie will bake longer after the filling is added, so it should not be completely browned at this point. Remove the pie dish from the oven, set it on a wire cooling rack, and remove the foil or parchment and pie weights. Keep the oven at 350°F.

3. MAKE THE FILLING: Thaw the plums in a colander placed inside a large bowl to collect the juices and set aside. Puree the blueberries in a food processor. Pour the blueberry puree into a 2-cup measuring cup. Add the vanilla, lemon juice, and enough of the plum juice to make 1½ cups. Pour the liquid into a medium saucepan. Stir in the tapioca starch and cornstarch along with the sugar, salt, and cinnamon. Bring the mixture to a boil to thicken it. (Note that the tapioca starch starts to thicken at a slightly lower temperature than cornstarch. You may notice streaks of thickened juice in the liquid—don't worry, this is the tapioca starch thickening first.) As the liquid comes to a boil, the cornstarch will thicken, too. The liquid will transform from thin and cloudy into a rich, clearer dark gel. Remove from the heat and fold in the thawed plums, then transfer this mixture to the partially blind-baked and still hot pie crust.

4. FINISH THE ASSEMBLY AND BAKE: Remove the frozen disc of topping from the freezer. Peel the silicone mat/parchment off the mold. Using your thumbs, carefully press the disc out from the tart ring and place it on the surface of the filled pie, smooth side facing up. Cover the edges of the pie with a pie crust shield and bake on the middle oven rack until the topping puffs a bit, browns slightly, and sets, about 35 minutes.

5. Remove the pie from the oven, place on a cooling rack, and allow the pie to cool completely, at least 4 hours.

6. DECORATE THE PIE: Brush aside all thoughts of eventual cleanup and fling spoonfuls of the purple Royal Icing across the top of the pie using a spoon and an almost carefree sense of joy. This pie should be served when it has cooled to room temperature. (Leftovers can be stored, covered, at room temperature for up to 3 days.)

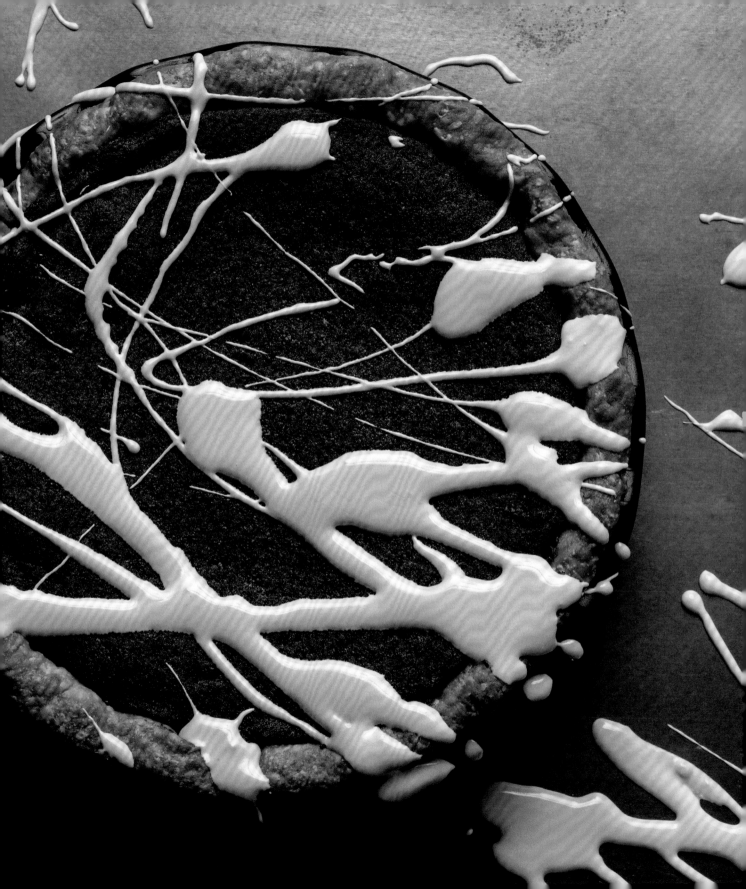

The NEW NUT PIES

When people think of nuts for pies, most people think of pecans. While pecans make a fantastic pie, the world of nut pies is so much larger than the mighty pecan! Macadamias, peanuts, and hazelnuts, among others, can all be used to bring fabulous flavors and distinct crunch to pies. In addition to being eminently adaptable, these nut pies keep for several days and are some of the easiest to transport because most don't require refrigeration and they tend to be sturdier than cream or fruit pies. Also, unlike seasonal fruits, nuts are available year-round in the grocery store, so there's no need to wait to try these recipes.

GERMAN CHOCOLATE
Pecan

MAKES ONE 9-INCH PIE

WHAT YOU NEED
- Pie dough for Cocoa Pastry Crust (page 40)
- 9-inch standard pie plate
- Pie crust shield or foil (see page 19)
- Plastic squeeze bottle or a piping bag (see page 21) fitted with a #2 piping tip

Did you know that German chocolate cake has no connection with the country of Germany? The cake was made using German's sweet chocolate, a baking chocolate developed by a man named Samuel German. Feel free to drop that trivia at your next party and impress your friends. The traditional German chocolate cake flavors—chocolate, caramel, coconut, nuts—are the inspiration for this award-winning pecan pie. The caramel-y custard filling is packed with toasted coconut and chocolate reminiscent of the filling and topping layers of a German chocolate cake.

1. PARTIALLY BLIND-BAKE THE CRUST: Follow the instructions on page 47. The pie will bake longer after the filling is added, so it should not be completely baked at this point. Remove the pie dish from the oven, set it on a wire cooling rack, and remove the foil or parchment and pie weights. Keep the oven at 350°F.

2. MAKE THE FILLING: Into the bowl of a food processor, place the dulce de leche, brown sugar, butter, corn syrup, eggs, flour, and salt. Process until uniformly mixed, about 10 seconds. Add the pecans, ¼ cup/0.75 ounce/21 grams of the coconut, and the chocolate chips. Pulse once or twice to just incorporate them into the filling.

3. FILL THE CRUST AND BAKE: Place a pie crust shield on the crust to protect the edges from drips and splashes and pour the mixture into the warm pie shell. Carefully transfer the filled pie to the oven and bake until the top has browned slightly and the filling has puffed and set, about 35 minutes. If the center still sloshes when the pie is moved, continue baking, checking every 5 minutes until the filling has puffed and the center wobbles slightly. Remove the pie from the oven, and cool completely before finishing.

INGREDIENT	VOLUME	WEIGHT (STANDARD)	WEIGHT (METRIC)
Dulce de leche	1¼ cups (from 1 13.4-ounce can)	13.4 ounces	380 grams
Dark brown sugar, lightly packed	1 cup	7 ounces	200 grams
Unsalted butter, softened	2 tablespoons	1 ounce	28 grams
Dark corn syrup	¼ cup	2.9 ounces	82 grams
Eggs	3 large		
All-purpose flour	1 tablespoon	0.3 ounce	9 grams
Salt	½ teaspoon		
Pecan pieces, toasted	2 cups	8 ounces	227 grams
Sweetened coconut flakes, toasted	½ cup	1.5 ounces	42 grams
Miniature semisweet chocolate chips	¼ cup	1.5 ounces	43 grams
Chocolate Ganache (page 264), warm and pourable	½ recipe		

4. TOP THE PIE: Add the warm Chocolate Ganache to the squeeze bottle or the prepared piping bag. Place the pie shield on again to keep the edges clean and drizzle the ganache generously over the surface of the pie. Sprinkle the remaining ¼ cup/0.75 ounce/21 grams toasted coconut evenly over the pie. This pie is best served and stored at room temperature. (Leftovers keep up to 3 days.)

Maple-y
WALNUT

MAKES ONE 9-INCH PIE

WHAT YOU NEED
- Pie dough for a Deep-Dish Single Crust (page 36)
- 9-inch standard pie plate
- Silicone maple leaf veiner (optional; see Sources, page 265)
- Fondant leaf veining tool (optional)
- 4¾-inch maple leaf cookie cutter
- Instant-read thermometer
- Pie crust shield or foil (see page 19)
- Plastic squeeze bottle with a narrow tip or a piping bag (see page 21) fitted with a #2 piping tip

We both grew up eating pancake syrup at breakfast time. We love the taste of pure maple syrup, but we still retain some affection for that in-your-face, over-the-top taste of "maple-flavored pancake syrup." Interestingly, the corn syrup in pancake syrup has an important chemical property; it is an invert sugar, meaning that it inherently resists crystallization. Original versions of this recipe used pure maple syrup but were not producing the gooey pie filling we were after. We realized that in order to produce the maple-walnut pie of our dreams, we had to use the maple-y syrup of our childhood—so purists, take note, and don't try to substitute real maple in this pie!

1. PREPARE THE CRUST AND DECORATION: Divide the pie dough into 2 discs, using about 85% of the dough to create 1 disc and 15% for the other. If you are using a scale (recommended!), the first piece should be 12.5 ounces/350 grams and the other piece should be 2.5 ounces/70 grams.

2. Roll out the largest portion of dough to a ⅛-inch thickness and place in a standard 9-inch pie pan. Crimp the edges as desired (page 24), then place the crust in the freezer until it is firm, about 20 minutes. Preheat the oven to 350°F.

3. To prepare the optional maple leaf decoration, roll out the smaller disc of dough to a ⅛-inch thickness. Press a large (about 4½ inches in diameter) silicone maple leaf veining tool onto the dough, using the rolling pin to ensure embossing. Peel off the tool and run a fondant veining tool along the leaf veins to reinforce the pattern in the dough.

recipe continues

INGREDIENT	VOLUME	WEIGHT (STANDARD)	WEIGHT (METRIC)
EGG WASH			
Egg yolk	1 large		
Heavy cream	1 tablespoon	0.5 ounce	15 grams
FILLING			
Walnut pieces	2½ cups	10 ounces	283 grams
Unsalted butter	6 tablespoons	3 ounces	85 grams
Light brown sugar, lightly packed	1 cup	7 ounces	200 grams
Salt	½ teaspoon		
Pancake syrup	¾ cup	8.25 ounces	234 grams
Maple extract	¼ teaspoon		
Eggs	3 large		
White chocolate chips	¼ cup	1.5 ounces	43 grams

INGREDIENT	VOLUME	WEIGHT (STANDARD)	WEIGHT (METRIC)
TOPPING			
Unsalted butter	1 tablespoon	0.5 ounce	14 grams
Confectioners' sugar	½ cup	2 ounces	57 grams
Pure maple syrup	2 tablespoons		
Salt	⅛ teaspoon		

Using a maple leaf cookie cutter (same size as the silicone tool), cut out a maple leaf shape. You can also make the veins of the maple leaf using a blunt tool like the back of a knife. Place the leaf in the freezer to firm for at least 10 minutes.

4. Stir the yolk and cream together to make an egg wash. Brush the top of the leaf with the egg wash and place it in the refrigerator until ready to use.

5. BEGIN MAKING THE FILLING: Place the walnuts on a sheet pan and bake until they are slightly darker and have a nutty aroma, about 7 minutes. Transfer them to a large mixing bowl and set aside.

6. PARTIALLY BLIND-BAKE THE CRUST: Follow the instructions on page 47. The pie will bake longer after the filling is added, so it should not be completely browned at this point. Remove the pie dish from the oven, set it on a wire cooling rack, and remove the foil or parchment and pie weights. Reduce the oven temperature to 275°F.

7. CONTINUE MAKING THE FILLING: When the crust is almost finished baking, melt the butter in a large microwave-safe bowl. Whisk in the brown sugar, salt, pancake syrup, and maple extract. Finally, whisk in the eggs one at a time.

8. Microwave the mixture at medium (50%) power, checking the temperature and stirring every minute or so until the mixture reaches 130°F, about 5 minutes (you can also heat the mixture using a double boiler on the stovetop; you will need to keep whisking it over a pan of simmering water—make sure the bottom of the bowl doesn't touch the water—until it reaches 130°F, about 10 minutes).

9. Pour the mixture through a fine-mesh sieve into the bowl of walnuts. Fold in the white chocolate chips.

10. FILL THE CRUST AND BAKE: Place a pie crust shield on the pie to protect the crust edges from drips and splashes and pour the mixture into the warm pie shell. Gently place the egg-washed leaf (if using) on the surface of the pie in the center.

11. Carefully transfer the filled pie to the middle rack of the oven and bake until the leaf is browned and the filling has puffed and set, about 55 minutes. If the center still sloshes when the pie is moved, continue baking, checking every 5 minutes until the filling has puffed and the center wobbles slightly. Remove the pie from the oven, take off the shield, and let the pie cool to room temperature before completing.

12. PREPARE THE TOPPING: Melt the butter in a small microwave-safe bowl. Whisk in the confectioners' sugar, maple syrup, and salt. Pour this warm glaze into a squeeze bottle or prepared piping bag. Place the pie shield on the pie again to keep the edges clean and place the silicone maple shape over the leaf to mask it. Drizzle the glaze decoratively over the surface of the pie. Remove the shield and silicone leaf. Serve immediately. (Leftovers can be stored, covered, at room temperature for up to 3 days.)

THE GUYS TALK PIES:
Flavor Inspirations

We take pride in the fact that many of our pie creations are flavors that haven't been seen too often (if ever) baked in a pie crust. Over the years, we've been asked how we come up with the ideas for some of our pies. Actually, we find inspiration in the foods we see every day. Ice cream flavors at the grocery store, the cocktail menu at the hip new restaurant, and candy bar aisle at the gas station are all places where we've been inspired to create a new pie. We keep our eyes open to what looks good to us, and we keep a list of flavors and flavor combinations that we would like to try in a pie one day. When the time comes to develop a new recipe, we pick a flavor from the list and think (a) how can we make this into a pie? and (b) how can we make this our own? Sometimes it's enough to turn a fun flavor into a pie that we've never seen in a pie before. If it's something we've seen before, we make sure to create it in a way that makes it our own. Sometimes that involves a fresh new take on a classic flavor by incorporating new flavors or techniques into making it. The world is full of inspiration for pie—keep an eye open and you will soon develop an unending list of ideas that you can't wait to turn into a new pie of your own!

Smoky
CARAMEL ALMOND

MAKES ONE 9-INCH PIE

WHAT YOU NEED
- Pie dough for a Standard Single Crust (page 35)
- 9-inch standard pie plate
- Pie crust shield or foil (see page 19)

This pie is all about scotch whisky from Islay, Scotland. Many of the whiskies produced in this part of the country have a characteristic taste of peat—a rich, smoky, campfire-like flavor that is so good for sipping on cold winter nights. If you favor the single malts, we suggest Laphroaig, or, for a blended scotch, the aptly named Big Peat. In this pie, the scotch is paired with the flavors of toasted almonds, dulce de leche, and caramelized white chocolate. Actual campfire not included.

1. PARTIALLY BLIND-BAKE THE CRUST: Follow the instructions on page 47. The pie will bake longer after the filling is added, so it should not be completely browned at this point. Remove the pie dish from the oven, set it on a wire cooling rack, and remove the foil or parchment and pie weights. Keep the oven at 350°F.

2. MAKE THE FILLING: Into the bowl of a food processor, place the scotch, dulce de leche, brown sugar, butter, cane syrup, eggs, flour, salt, and vanilla. Process until uniformly mixed. Add the almonds and pulse once or twice until just incorporated into the filling.

3. FILL THE CRUST AND BAKE: Place a pie shield on the crust to protect the edges from drips and splashes and pour the mixture into the warm pie shell. Carefully transfer the filled pie to the oven and bake until the top has browned slightly and the filling has puffed and set, 40 to 45 minutes.

recipe continues

INGREDIENT	VOLUME	WEIGHT (STANDARD)	WEIGHT (METRIC)
FILLING			
Islay scotch whisky	1 tablespoon	0.45 ounce	13 grams
Dulce de leche	1¼ cups (from 1 13.4-ounce can)	13.4 ounces	380 grams
Light brown sugar, lightly packed	1 cup	7 ounces	200 grams
Unsalted butter, softened	2 tablespoons	1 ounce	28 grams
Cane syrup, such as Steen's (see Sources, page 265)	¼ cup	3 ounces	85 grams
Eggs	3 large		
All-purpose flour	1 tablespoon		
Salt	½ teaspoon		
Vanilla extract	1 teaspoon		
Sliced almonds, toasted	3⅓ cups	10 ounces	283 grams
TOPPING			
White chocolate, finely chopped		4 ounces	113 grams
Heavy cream	¼ cup plus 2 teaspoons	2.3 ounces	65 grams
Islay scotch whisky	2 teaspoons		
Salt	pinch		
Smoked whole almonds	12		

If the center still sloshes when the pie is moved, continue baking, checking every 5 minutes until the filling has puffed and the center wobbles slightly.

4. Remove the pie from the oven and place it on a wire cooling rack. Decrease the oven temperature to 250°F.

5. **PREPARE THE TOPPING:** Place the white chocolate in a 9-inch round cake pan and place in the oven for 30 minutes, stirring every 10 minutes with a rubber spatula. The white chocolate will melt, then brown and appear crumbly. Remove the pan from the oven.

6. Heat the cream in the microwave for about 1 minute, until just starting to boil. Stir in the scotch and salt, and then pour into the cake pan while stirring with a rubber spatula. Keep stirring and smearing the caramelized chocolate crumbles against the pan until the chocolate is melted and incorporated into the cream. Strain the caramelized white chocolate ganache through a fine-mesh sieve into a measuring cup with a spout. Pour the strained ganache over the pie. Arrange the smoked almonds evenly around the circumference of the pie surface at the positions of the clock, to designate individual servings.

7. This pie should be served when both the filling and the topping have cooled to room temperature. (Leftovers can be stored, covered, at room temperature for up to 3 days.)

HUNKY MONKEY

Peanut

MAKES ONE 9-INCH PIE

WHAT YOU NEED

- Pie dough for a Standard Single Crust (page 35)
- 9-inch standard pie plate
- Instant-read thermometer
- Pie crust shield or foil (see page 19)
- Plastic squeeze bottle with a narrow tip or a piping bag (see page 21) fitted with a #2 piping tip

David Lebovitz's roasted banana ice cream recipe involves roasting the bananas to remove liquid, softening the fruit, and caramelizing the sugars—a relatively easy way to produce rich and concentrated banana flavor. We enjoyed the ice cream so much that we wondered if we could use the rich banana flavor in a pie, too. We adapted David's method of concentrating the banana flavor, then added it to the caramel-y matrix of a nut pie. Dark chocolate provides the perfect counterpoint to the sweet bananas and peanuts. After loving the final recipe, we still needed a name. Thinking on it, we realized that the combination of bananas, chocolate, and nuts should remind you of that classic combination from those famous ice cream guys in Vermont.

1. PARTIALLY BLIND-BAKE THE CRUST: Follow the instructions on page 47. The pie will bake longer after the filling is added, so it should not be completely browned at this point. Remove the pie dish from the oven, set it on a wire cooling rack, and remove the foil or parchment and pie weights. Decrease the oven temperature to 275°F.

2. PREPARE THE FILLING: While the crust is blind-baking, melt 1 tablespoon/0.5 ounce/14 grams of the butter in a nonstick skillet along with ¼ cup/1.75 ounces/50 grams of the turbinado sugar over medium-high heat. Once the butter is melted, add the bananas, cover the pan, reduce the heat to low, and simmer for 10 minutes.

3. Uncover the pan. The bananas should have softened and look like they are sitting in a pool of liquid, with all the sugar dissolved. If not, turn the heat up a bit, re-cover the pan, and keep checking every 2 minutes until the liquid has released and the sugar has dissolved. Increase the heat to medium-high, keeping the liquid at the boiling point. Keep stirring with a rubber spatula, pressing on the bananas until they soften into a paste and the liquid has completely evaporated.

recipe continues

INGREDIENT	VOLUME	WEIGHT (STANDARD)	WEIGHT (METRIC)
Unsalted butter	6 tablespoons	3 ounces	85 grams
Turbinado sugar	1 cup plus 1 tablespoon	7.5 ounces	213 grams
Bananas, peeled and sliced (weighed after peeling)	about 4 medium	14 ounces	400 grams
Salt	½ teaspoon		
Lyle's Golden Syrup (see Sources, page 265)	¾ cup	8.25 ounces	234 grams
Eggs	3 large		
Vanilla extract	1 tablespoon	0.45 ounce	13 grams
Roasted unsalted peanuts	2½ cups	10 ounces	283 grams
Miniature chocolate chips	½ cup	3 ounces	85 grams
Chocolate Ganache (page 264), warm and pourable	½ recipe		

The bananas will start to caramelize and concentrate. Keep breaking up and flipping the banana paste until fully caramelized and concentrated, another 10 to 15 minutes, then remove it from the heat. You should have approximately 1½ cups/7.6–8.8 ounces/215–250 grams of caramelized banana paste at this point. Set it aside.

4. Melt the remaining 5 tablespoons/2.5 ounces/71 grams butter in a microwave-safe bowl. Whisk in the remaining ¾ cup plus 1 tablespoon/ 5.75 ounces/163 grams turbinado sugar, salt, and golden syrup. Whisk in the eggs one at a time, mixing well between each addition. Microwave the mixture at medium (50%) power, checking the temperature and stirring every minute or so until it gets to 130°F. (You can also use a double boiler; to do so, fill a medium saucepan with 1 inch of water, bring the water to a simmer over medium-high heat, then reduce the heat to medium-low and set the bowl over the water, making sure the bottom of the bowl doesn't touch the water; whisk constantly until it reaches 130°F on an instant-read thermometer, about 10 minutes.)

5. Pour the mixture through a fine-mesh sieve and into another bowl to remove any stray bits of cooked egg. Whisk in the vanilla and the caramelized banana paste. Switch to a rubber spatula and fold in the roasted peanuts and the chocolate chips.

6. FILL THE CRUST AND BAKE: Place a pie crust shield on the crust to protect the edges from drips and splashes and pour the mixture into the warm pie shell. Transfer the filled pie with the pie shield to the middle rack of the oven and bake until the top has browned slightly and the filling has puffed and set, about 1 hour and 10 minutes. If the center still sloshes when the pie is moved, continue baking, checking every 5 minutes until the filling has puffed and the center wobbles slightly. Remove the pie from the oven, take off the pie shield, and set the pie on a wire rack to cool completely.

7. DECORATE THE PIE: Pour the warm Chocolate Ganache into a squeeze bottle or prepared piping bag. Place the shield on the pie again to keep the edges clean, and drizzle the ganache decoratively over the surface. The pie is best served at room temperature. (Leftovers can be stored, covered, at room temperature, for up to 3 days.)

THE GUYS TALK PIES:
Pie-Proofing Your Oven

Having baked pies in many different ovens over the years, there are three things we always check for before we use an oven: temperature accuracy, hot spots, and tilt. Place an oven thermometer in the center of the oven and heat the oven to a desired temperature. Check the temperature 15 to 20 minutes after the oven has indicated that it has reached that temperature. Ideally, the temperature on the oven and the thermometer will match. Hot spots can be found by placing about 15 slices of white bread across one of the racks of the oven and toasting them. The goal is for all slices to turn evenly golden brown at the same time. If some burn, that indicates a hot spot in the oven. Tilt is especially important for pies with baked custard fillings, like the German Chocolate Pecan (page 142). If the oven or oven rack is not level, the filling will be higher on one side than the other and could bake unevenly or cause one side to dry out while the other side remains undercooked. Check your oven racks with a carpenter's level to ensure the rack is level both side to side and front to back. If your oven has any of these imperfections, clearly you must destroy it, claim the insurance money, and buy a new one. No, don't do that! Just call an appliance technician and ask to have your oven calibrated and leveled. Otherwise, fold up squares of aluminum foil to use as shims to prop up the "low" side of the pie pan so as to even out the slope, adjust the set temperature on the oven to compensate for the temperature discrepancy, and rotate your pies a bit more frequently than you normally would to minimize the effects of hot spots.

Malted
CHOCOLATE HAZELNUT

MAKES ONE 9-INCH PIE

WHAT YOU NEED
- Pie dough for a Standard Single Crust (page 35)
- 9-inch standard pie plate
- Instant-read thermometer
- Pie crust shield or foil (see page 19)

A malted milkshake from the olde soda shoppe. A box of Whoppers at the drive-in movie. Or Ralphie's favorite, a glass of Ovaltine, complete with decoder pin and crummy commercials! The flavor of malt brings a sense of nostalgic comfort to many desserts. We've resurrected good old malted milk from the 1950s and paired it with dark chocolate and toasted hazelnuts to create a rich, retro-modern treat (isn't that the best kind?).

1. PARTIALLY BLIND-BAKE THE CRUST: Follow the instructions on page 47. The pie will bake longer after the filling is added, so it should not be completely browned at this point. Remove the pie dish from the oven, set it on a wire cooling rack, and remove the foil or parchment and pie weights. Decrease the oven temperature to 275°F.

2. MAKE THE FILLING: When the crust is almost finished blind-baking, melt the butter in a large microwave-safe bowl. Whisk in the brown sugar, salt, and both syrups. Whisk in the eggs one at a time, mixing well between each addition. Microwave the mixture at medium (50%) power, checking the temperature and stirring every minute or so until it gets to 130°F. (You can also use a double boiler; to do so, fill a medium saucepan with 1 inch of water, bring the water to a simmer over medium-high heat, then reduce the heat to medium-low and set the bowl over the water, making sure the bottom of the bowl doesn't touch the water; whisk constantly until it reaches 130°F on an instant-read thermometer, about 10 minutes.)

recipe continues

INGREDIENT	VOLUME	WEIGHT (STANDARD)	WEIGHT (METRIC)
FILLING			
Unsalted butter	6 tablespoons	3 ounces	85 grams
Light brown sugar, lightly packed	1 cup	7 ounces	200 grams
Salt	½ teaspoon		
Barley malt extract syrup	⅓ cup	4 ounces	113 grams
Light corn syrup	⅓ cup	4 ounces	113 grams
Eggs	3 large		
Blanched, roasted, unsalted hazelnuts, coarsely chopped	2½ cups	10 ounces	283 grams
Bittersweet chocolate chips	½ cup	3 ounces	85 grams
MALTED GANACHE TOPPING			
Malted milk powder	¼ cup	1 ounce	28 grams
Heavy cream	¼ cup	2 ounces	57 grams
Bittersweet chocolate chips	⅓ cup	2 ounces	57 grams

3. Pour the mixture through a fine-mesh sieve into another bowl to remove any stray bits of cooked egg. Fold the hazelnuts and chocolate chips into the egg mixture, stirring until the chocolate chips are melted. Place a pie crust shield on the pie to protect the edges from drips and splashes and pour the mixture into the warm pie shell. The hazelnuts will all float to the surface—this is okay.

4. BAKE THE PIE: Carefully transfer the filled pie to the middle oven rack and bake until the surface has browned slightly and the filling has puffed and set, about 60 minutes. If the center is still sloshy, continue baking, checking every 5 minutes, until it has puffed and the center barely jiggles. Remove the pie crust shield and allow the pie to cool completely.

5. MAKE THE MALTED GANACHE TOPPING: Place the malted milk powder and cream in a small microwave-safe bowl and stir the cream to dissolve the powder. Microwave the cream on high for 1 to 2 minutes, until it just starts to boil. Add the chocolate chips and stir until melted and the mixture is uniform. Pour the ganache over the surface of the cooled pie. You may need to tilt the pie to encourage the ganache to flow across the whole surface of the pie or use an offset spatula to spread it to the pie crust edge. The ganache will set as it cools at room temperature. The pie is best served at room temperature. (Leftovers can be stored, covered, at room temperature for up to 3 days.)

THE GUYS TALK PIES:

But ya ARE
Blanch-ing Hazelnuts

Baking can be a lot of work, and when we can eliminate unnecessary steps, we do. Fortunately, one of the farmers' markets near where we live has an incredible source of nuts of all kinds, including hazelnuts that come already blanched and roasted. However, we know that the average American supermarket stocks only raw hazelnuts that still have their brown skins attached, so a little extra prep is needed. Blanching and roasting hazelnuts is relatively simple, but it does take some manual labor.

Scatter the raw hazelnuts on a sheet pan and roast them in a preheated 350°F oven, tossing them every 5 minutes, until the skins have split and blistered, 10 to 15 minutes. Immediately transfer the hot nuts to a thick kitchen towel. Wrap the nuts in the towel and allow them to steam for about 10 minutes to help loosen the skins. Vigorously rub the hazelnuts between the layers of the towel to remove the skins. Not all of the skins will come off, but that's okay. To roast the nuts for additional flavor, return the skinned nuts to the pan and bake until the nuts are golden brown and fragrant, about 5 minutes.

PISTACHIO,
Honey

MAKES ONE 9-INCH PIE

WHAT YOU NEED
- Pie dough for a Standard Single Crust (page 35)
- 9-inch standard pie plate
- Instant-read thermometer
- Pie crust shield or foil (see page 19)

Our version of baklava, the sticky dessert popular in the Mediterranean and Middle East, pairs pistachios and honey with lemon and cardamom for a modern take on a classic treat. While the bottom is our standard crust, the topping of crisped, flaky layers of phyllo dough reflects the origins of this pie.

1. PARTIALLY BLIND-BAKE THE CRUST: Follow the instructions on page 47. The pie will bake longer after the filling is added, so it should not be completely browned at this point. Remove the pie dish from the oven, set it on a wire cooling rack, and remove the foil or parchment and pie weights. Decrease the oven temperature to 275°F.

2. MAKE THE FILLING: When the crust is almost finished blind-baking, use a medium microwave-safe bowl and whisk together the melted butter, sugar, salt, honey, corn syrup, lemon zest, lemon juice, cardamom, and cinnamon. Whisk in the eggs one at a time, mixing well between each addition. Microwave the mixture at medium (50%) power, checking the temperature and stirring every minute or so until it gets to 130°F. (You can also use a double boiler; to do so, fill a medium saucepan with 1 inch of water, bring the water to a simmer over medium-high heat, then reduce the heat to medium-low and set

recipe continues

INGREDIENT	VOLUME	WEIGHT (STANDARD)	WEIGHT (METRIC)
FILLING			
Unsalted butter, melted	6 tablespoons	3 ounces	85 grams
Sugar	1 cup	7 ounces	200 grams
Salt	½ teaspoon		
Honey	⅓ cup	4 ounces	113 grams
Light corn syrup	⅓ cup	4 ounces	113 grams
Finely grated lemon zest	1 teaspoon		
Fresh lemon juice	1 tablespoon	0.5 ounce	14 grams
Ground cardamom	¼ teaspoon		
Ground cinnamon	¼ teaspoon		
Eggs	3 large		
Pistachios, shelled, roasted, unsalted, and coarsely chopped	1¾ cups	10 ounces	283 grams
TOPPING			
Phyllo dough, thawed	3 sheets		
Unsalted butter, melted	1½ tablespoons	0.75 ounce	21 grams
Sugar	2 teaspoons		

the bowl over the water, making sure the bottom of the bowl doesn't touch the water; whisk constantly until it reaches 130°F on an instant-read thermometer, about 10 minutes.)

3. **FILL THE CRUST:** Fold the pistachios into the filling. Place a pie crust shield on the pie to protect the edges from drips and splashes and pour the mixture into the warm pie shell.

4. **MAKE THE TOPPING:** Place 1 sheet of phyllo on the countertop and brush with melted butter. Sprinkle with 1 teaspoon sugar and cover with a second sheet of phyllo. Brush that sheet with melted butter and sprinkle with the other teaspoon of sugar. Place the third sheet of phyllo on top and gently press the dough all over to seal. Place a 9-inch circle (such as a cake pan, a plate, or a circle cut from cardboard or parchment) on top. Using a sharp knife or pizza wheel, trim away the excess phyllo from around the circle. Remove the cake pan and slice the circle into 8 even wedges (like a pie). Place the phyllo wedges slightly overlapping around the surface of the pie.

5. **BAKE THE PIE:** Carefully transfer the filled pie to the middle rack of the oven and bake until the phyllo wedges have browned, crisped, and puffed, and the filling is set, about 60 minutes. If the center still sloshes when the pie is moved, continue baking, checking every 5 minutes until the filling has puffed and the center wobbles slightly. Allow the pie to cool completely at room temperature before serving. (Leftovers can be stored, covered, at room temperature for up to 3 days.)

LEFTOVER PHYLLO DOUGH

You've probably figured out by now that there are way more sheets of phyllo dough in a box than just the three you used for the pie topping in this pie. If you weren't already planning on having spanakopita for dinner on the day you have the pie for dessert, you may be wondering what to do with the extra. Fortunately, phyllo can be re-wrapped and re-frozen for future use. In addition to savory pies for dinner, you can use the same three-layered phyllo topping trick for other baked pies—say, if your top lattice isn't working out or you forgot to make enough dough for a top crust; just pull the leftover phyllo out of the freezer for a quick fix.

Toasted
MACADAMIA

MAKES ONE 9-INCH PIE
WHAT YOU NEED
- Pie dough for a Standard Single Crust (page 35)
- 9-inch standard pie plate
- Instant-read thermometer
- Pie crust shield or foil (see page 19)
- Piping bag (see page 21) fitted with a Wilton #1M or other large star piping tip (optional)

When using fancy ingredients, you want to let them shine—not cover them up with lots of other ingredients. For example, caviar is best humbly served on a blini with crème fraîche, while a few thin shavings of truffle effortlessly dress up a simple pasta dish. Although not as pricy as caviar or truffles, macadamia nuts are a flavorful, high-end ingredient that needs no grand frills or flourishes. These buttery nuts shine in this pie, accented with a few wisps of nutmeg and dark rum for a luxurious delight.

1. PARTIALLY BLIND-BAKE THE CRUST: Follow the instructions on page 47. The pie will bake longer after the filling is added, so it should not be completely browned at this point. Remove the pie dish from the oven, set it on a wire cooling rack, and remove the foil or parchment and pie weights. Keep the oven at 350°F.

2. MAKE THE FRANGIPANE: Spread the nuts on a baking sheet and lightly toast them in the oven, 6 to 9 minutes. Remove them from the oven and allow them to cool slightly for 5 minutes. Place half the macadamia nuts into the bowl of a food processor and pulse a few times, until the nuts are mostly chopped. Add the granulated sugar and continue to pulse until the nuts are finely ground. Add the butter, egg, rum, nutmeg, flour, and salt and process until evenly combined. Add the remaining nuts to the filling mixture and pulse once or twice until they are just incorporated into the mixture.

recipe continues

INGREDIENT	VOLUME	WEIGHT (STANDARD)	WEIGHT (METRIC)
FRANGIPANE			
Raw macadamia nuts	1⅓ cups	7 ounces	200 grams
Granulated sugar	½ cup	3.5 ounces	100 grams
Unsalted butter, at room temperature	3 tablespoons	1.5 ounces	43 grams
Egg	1 large		
Dark rum	1 tablespoon	0.45 ounce	13 grams
Ground nutmeg	1 teaspoon		
All-purpose flour	1 tablespoon	0.3 ounce	9 grams
Salt	¼ teaspoon		
CINNAMON SUGAR MERINGUE TOPPING			
Egg whites	3 large		
Light brown sugar, lightly packed	⅔ cup	4.65 ounces	133 grams
Salt	⅛ teaspoon		
Vanilla extract	½ teaspoon		
Ground cinnamon	½ teaspoon		
Raw macadamia nuts	about 12	1 ounce	28 grams

3. FILL THE CRUST AND BAKE: Place a pie crust shield on the pie to protect the edges from drips and pour the mixture into the warm pie shell. Place the pie in the oven on the middle rack and bake until it is puffed and browned, and no longer jiggles when jostled, about 15 minutes. Remove the pie from the oven and immediately start preparing the meringue topping.

4. MAKE THE CINNAMON SUGAR MERINGUE TOPPING: Combine the egg whites, brown sugar, and salt in the bowl of a stand mixer. Place the bowl over a pot of simmering water to create a water bath. Cook the egg white mixture over the simmering water, whisking constantly until the temperature on an instant-read thermometer reaches 160°F. Transfer the bowl to a stand mixer fitted with the whisk attachment and beat on medium-high until the meringue holds medium peaks, about 8 minutes. Beat in the vanilla and cinnamon. Spread or decoratively pipe the meringue over the still warm surface of the pie.

5. DECORATE THE PIE: Carefully slice the raw macadamia nuts into approximate quarters. Try to avoid generating too much nut dust. Sprinkle the large chunks of chopped macadamia nuts on top of the pie, leaving the dust behind—which would burn if you used it. Place the pie back in the oven on the middle rack for 5 minutes. Now turn the broiler on high for 20 seconds to 1 minute. Do not take your eyes off the pie! The intensity of broilers varies, and what takes ours 45 seconds could take yours 20 seconds. Remove the pie when the meringue and nuts just start to brown slightly and cool the pie completely at room temperature before serving. (Leftovers can be stored in the refrigerator up to 2 days.)

GINGERBREAD

Cashew

MAKES ONE 9½-INCH DEEP-DISH PIE
WHAT YOU NEED
• Pie dough for a Gingerbread Crust (page 37)
• 9½-inch deep-dish pie plate
• 2-inch gingerbread man cookie cutter
• Pie crust shield or foil (see page 19)
• Piping bag (see page 21) fitted with a #3 piping tip, if decorating with royal icing

There are gingerbread houses, gingerbread cookies, and gingerbread cakes. We think it's high time for a gingerbread pie. Our basic pie crust is augmented with gingerbread elements, while the filling features the dark, bittersweet taste of molasses, along with warm spices including the zing of two types of ginger. This wintertime classic combination of flavors is elevated by the addition of crisp, toasty cashews. Cashews' curvy shape reminds us of the cute squiggles used to decorate gingerbread men (and ladies) adorning the top of the pie.

1. PREPARE THE CRUST: Roll out the large disc of dough to a ⅛-inch thickness (page 42) and place in a deep-dish pie plate—ideally, one with deep ruffled edges. Trim the dough along the ruffled edges or crimp as desired (see page 24). Place the prepared crust in the freezer until it is quite firm, about 20 minutes. Preheat the oven to 350°F.

2. PARTIALLY BLIND-BAKE THE CRUST: Follow the instructions on page 47. The pie will bake longer after the filling is added, so it should not be completely browned at this point. Remove the pie dish from the oven, set it on a wire cooling rack, and remove the foil or parchment and pie weights. Keep the oven at 350°F.

3. Roll the small disc of dough to a ¹⁄₁₆-inch thickness and transfer it to a piece of parchment. Using the gingerbread man cutter, cut out about 10 gingerbread men. Slide the parchment with the gingerbread cutouts onto a sheet pan and place the little guys in the freezer.

INGREDIENT	VOLUME	WEIGHT (STANDARD)	WEIGHT (METRIC)
FILLING			
Dulce de leche	1¼ cups (from 1 13.4-ounce can)	13.4 ounces	380 grams
Muscovado sugar	1⅓ cups	9.3 ounces	265 grams
Unsalted butter, at room temperature	3 tablespoons	1.5 ounces	43 grams
Unsulphured molasses	⅓ cup	3.75 ounces	106 grams
Eggs	4 large		
All-purpose flour	4 teaspoons	0.4 ounce	12 grams
Kosher salt	¾ teaspoon		
Ground ginger	1½ teaspoons		
Ground cinnamon	1¼ teaspoons		
Ground cloves	¼ teaspoon		
Crystallized ginger, chopped	¼ cup	1.4 ounces	40 grams
Cashews, roughly chopped and toasted	3 cups	13 ounces	369 grams
DECORATION			
White Royal Icing (page 259), piping consistency (optional)	1 recipe		

4. MAKE THE FILLING: To the bowl of a food processor, add the dulce de leche, muscovado sugar, butter, molasses, eggs, flour, salt, ginger, cinnamon, cloves, and crystallized ginger. Process until uniformly mixed. If the bowl of your food processor is large enough, add the cashews and pulse once or twice until just incorporated into the filling. (If you have a small food processor, you'll have to stir the mixture and cashews together in a larger bowl.)

5. Place a pie crust shield on the crust to protect the edges from drips and splashes and pour the mixture into the warm pie shell. Place the frozen gingerbread men from the freezer on the surface of the pie. You can arrange as many men as desired in whatever pattern you like, depending on the size of your cutter. Seven of them will fit nicely around the edge, arms outstretched but not quite holding hands.

6. BAKE THE PIE: Carefully transfer the filled pie to the middle rack of the oven and bake until the top has browned slightly and the filling has puffed and set, about 1 hour. The gingerbread men will also appear a bit more suntanned than when they went in. If the center is still jiggly, continue baking, checking every 5 minutes until it has set and is firm. Allow the pie to cool completely to room temperature.

7. ADD THE DECORATION: If desired, decorate the surface of the pie and the gingerbread men with the Royal Icing, using the prepared piping bag or a squeeze bottle if you prefer. This pie is best served at room temperature. (Leftovers can be stored, covered, at room temperature for up to 3 days.)

The NEW COCKTAIL PIES

Let's hope you have a well-stocked liquor cabinet. Not just for these pies, but in general. We're looking out for you and want you to be happy. If the cupboard is bare and you want to make these pies, a trip to the liquor store is in your future. Have fun! Or try that flask in Grandma's purse. Not sure what exactly is in there, but it never seems to be empty and it keeps a smile on her face. Just be sure to offer her a slice of pie in return.

STRAWBERRY MARGARITA

with Salted Rim

MAKES ONE 9-INCH PIE

WHAT YOU NEED

- Standard Single Crust (page 35), baked and cooled in a 9-inch standard pie plate
- Large-flake sea salt, such as Maldon, for serving

Chris's willpower is no match for the lure of an icy strawberry margarita. Its bright berry flavor with tart lime and a hint of orange beg to be made into a pie. For this creation, a strawberry cream filling made with a nonalcoholic frozen drink mixer is topped with lime curd and infused with a hint of tequila. A salted pie crust rim and a dusting of flaked sea salt sprinkled on the top just before serving is the perfect pairing for this sliceable cocktail. If you want this to be a completely alcohol-free pie, replace the tequila with orange juice.

1. MAKE THE SALTED RIM: Preheat the oven to 350°F. In a small bowl, whisk the egg white, then use a pastry brush to lightly coat a 2- to 3-inch section of the crust's edge with the egg white. Immediately sprinkle the brushed area with the sea salt. Continue around the pie until all of the edge has been brushed and sprinkled with salt. Don't brush the pie edge all at once; if your kitchen is warm or dry, the egg white may dry before you have a chance to sprinkle the salt. Bake the crust until the egg white is dry and the salt is set, 3 to 5 minutes. Transfer the pie crust to a wire rack to cool completely, about 15 minutes. You can use a dry pastry brush and a spoon like a broom and dustpan to collect any extra salt that may have landed inside the crust. (A few pieces of extra salt won't hurt, but a lot of salt could wreak havoc with your filling.)

2. MAKE THE STRAWBERRY CREAM FILLING: In a medium saucepan, whisk together the thawed strawberry drink mixer, orange juice, and cornstarch until the cornstarch is dissolved. Whisk in the egg yolks, condensed milk, and salt. Over medium heat, bring the mixture to a boil, whisking constantly. Continue whisking, reduce the heat to medium-low, and continue to boil for 1 minute.

recipe continues

INGREDIENT	VOLUME	WEIGHT (STANDARD)	WEIGHT (METRIC)
SALTED RIM			
Egg white, at room temperature	1 large		
Large-flake sea salt, such as Maldon	1 tablespoon	0.35 ounce	10 grams
STRAWBERRY CREAM FILLING			
Frozen strawberry daiquiri mixer (nonalcoholic), thawed	1¼ cups	10 ounces	283 grams
Fresh orange juice	2 tablespoons	1 ounce	28 grams
Cornstarch	3 tablespoons	0.8 ounce	23 grams
Egg yolks	3 large		
Sweetened condensed milk	1 14-ounce can	14 ounces	397 grams
Salt	pinch		
Unsalted butter	2 tablespoons	1 ounce	28 grams
Tequila	2 teaspoons		

INGREDIENT	VOLUME	WEIGHT (STANDARD)	WEIGHT (METRIC)
LIME CURD TOPPING			
Whole milk	1 tablespoon		
Unflavored powdered gelatin	½ teaspoon		
Finely grated lime zest	1 tablespoon		
Sugar	¾ cup	5.25 ounces	150 grams
Fresh lime juice	¼ cup	2 ounces	57 grams
Eggs	2 large		
Salt	pinch		
Unsalted butter, cut into 4 pieces	4 tablespoons	2 ounces	57 grams
Tequila	1 tablespoon	0.5 ounce	14 grams

3. Remove the saucepan from the heat and whisk in the butter and tequila until the butter has melted and is incorporated. Strain the mixture through a fine-mesh sieve into a medium bowl, using a rubber spatula to press the cream through the sieve.

4. Transfer the strawberry mixture to the cooled pie crust and smooth the top with an offset spatula. Press plastic wrap directly onto the top of the strawberry mixture and refrigerate until cool and firm throughout, at least 2 hours.

5. MAKE THE LIME CURD TOPPING: Place the milk in a small bowl. Sprinkle the gelatin evenly over the milk and set aside.

6. Combine the lime zest and sugar in a small saucepan. Using your fingertips, pinch the lime zest into the sugar to extract the flavorful lime oils. Do this until the sugar has turned a light green color. Whisk in the lime juice, eggs, and salt and cook over medium-low heat, stirring constantly, until the mixture begins to thicken and coats the back of a spoon. Watch the mixture carefully as it cooks, as it can thicken quickly. (If the mixture begins to bubble at the edges, immediately remove it from the heat.) When the mixture is thickened, remove the pan from the heat and whisk in the butter until melted and incorporated. Whisk in the softened gelatin and the tequila.

7. Remove the plastic wrap from the cold strawberry filling, and pour the lime mixture over the top, spreading evenly with an offset spatula, if needed.

8. CHILL THE PIE: Refrigerate the pie until it is cold, at least 3 more hours or up to overnight. Serve each slice with an additional light sprinkling of flaked sea salt. (The additional salt is not required, but it is highly recommended!) (Store leftovers tightly covered in the refrigerator for up to 2 days. Keep in mind that moisture in the air, especially if you live in a humid environment, will begin to dissolve the salt on the crust.)

CHERRY MANHATTANS,
Served Up

MAKES 8 INDIVIDUAL PIES
WHAT YOU NEED
• Large piping bag (see page 21)
• 8 4-ounce martini glasses

Mini pies! These individual cocktail-inspired pies have a fully cooked crumb crust of toasted graham crackers and browned butter, and they are already individually portioned for your guests. No half slices for you—everyone gets a whole one. Whiskey-and-vermouth–soaked cherries are folded into a creamy mousse, transforming the classic cocktail into a neoclassic dessert.

1. PREPARE THE CRUST: In a small (preferably *not* nonstick) saucepan, toast the graham cracker crumbs over medium heat, stirring constantly, until they are slightly darker and smell toasty, about 5 minutes. Transfer them to a medium bowl.

2. Add the butter to the same hot pan. Swirl the pan over medium heat until the butter has browned and has a nutty aroma, about 5 minutes, stirring or swirling constantly. Off the heat, stir in the granulated sugar and salt, then scrape this mixture into the bowl with the toasted crumbs and stir until evenly mixed.

recipe continues

INGREDIENT	VOLUME	WEIGHT (STANDARD)	WEIGHT (METRIC)
CRUST			
Graham cracker crumbs (from 14½ sheets)	1¾ cups plus 2 tablespoons	7.6 ounces	215 grams
Unsalted butter	7 tablespoons	3.5 ounces	99 grams
Granulated sugar	3 tablespoons	1.3 ounces	38 grams
Salt	pinch		
FILLING			
Rye whiskey	⅓ cup	2.35 ounces	67 grams
Sweet vermouth	2 tablespoons	1 ounce	28 grams
Angostura bitters	2 teaspoons		
Dried sour cherries	3 cups	16 ounces	454 grams
Unflavored powdered gelatin	1½ teaspoons		
Whole milk	½ cup	4.25 ounces	121 grams
Turbinado sugar	¼ cup	1.75 ounces	50 grams
Salt	¼ teaspoon		
Butterscotch baking chips	½ cup	3 ounces	85 grams
Heavy cream	1 cup	8.2 ounces	232 grams
TOPPING			
Heavy cream	½ cup	4.1 ounces	116 grams
Confectioners' sugar	1 tablespoon	0.25 ounce	7 grams
Maraschino cherries, drained and blotted dry	8		

3. Divide this mixture equally among eight 4-ounce martini glasses (really, any glass you would serve a pudding in works—be it a ramekin or rocks glass), 3 to 4 tablespoons (40 grams) of crumb mixture per glass. Using your fingers, press the crumb mixture into a thin, compact layer along the inside surface of the glasses, extending to about ½ inch from the top. Place the 8 glasses on a tray and put them in the refrigerator.

4. MAKE THE FILLING: Pour the whiskey, vermouth, and bitters into a small saucepan. Add the cherries and bring the mixture to a simmer. Turn off the heat, cover the pan, and let the fruits steam for 10 minutes. Transfer the fruit mixture to the bowl of a food processor and puree.

5. Sprinkle the gelatin over 2 tablespoons/1.05 ounces/30 grams of the milk in a small bowl; set aside.

6. In a medium saucepan, combine the remaining 6 tablespoons/ 3.2 ounces/91 grams of milk, the turbinado sugar, and salt. Cook over medium heat until the sugar is dissolved, about 3 minutes. Reduce the heat to medium-low, add the butterscotch chips, and cook, stirring often, until the chips are completely melted, about 5 minutes. Remove the saucepan from the heat and stir in the gelatin mixture until it is completely melted, about 1 minute.

7. Strain the mixture through a fine-mesh sieve into a large heat-safe bowl (this ensures no unmelted chunks of butterscotch or gelatin make it into the pie). Stir the pureed cherry mixture into the bowl. Allow the mixture to cool to room temperature, about 20 minutes, stirring occasionally.

8. Whip the cream until it holds stiff peaks, 1 to 3 minutes. Fold the cream into the cooled cherry mixture, and then transfer this filling to the piping bag. Cut the tip off the end of the piping bag, remove the martini glasses from the refrigerator, and fill them with the Manhattan cherry filling. The filling should extend above the graham layer but not quite to the tops of the glasses in order to save room for the whipped cream. Using a small offset spatula, smooth the tops.

9. MAKE THE TOPPING: Whip the cream with the confectioners' sugar until it holds stiff peaks, 1 to 3 minutes. Spread a dollop of whipped cream across the surface of the first Manhattan. Using the edge of a long straight spatula, scrape across the rim of the glass, removing the excess whipped cream and leaving a smooth white surface level with the rim of the glass. Repeat this process for the other 7 glasses.

10. Return the tray of cocktail pies to the refrigerator and chill until they are completely cold, at least 4 hours or up to 3 days. Garnish each "Manhattan" with a single maraschino cherry before serving.

The NICOLÉ

MAKES ONE 9½-INCH DEEP-DISH PIE
WHAT YOU NEED
• Cocoa Graham Cracker Crust (page 50), baked and cooled in a 9½-inch deep-dish pie plate with no lip
• Piping bag (see page 21) fitted with a decorative tip, such as a St. Honoré

There is a small Italian restaurant tucked away on a side street in St. Thomas that serves a wonderfully warm dessert cocktail made with coffee, chocolate, cinnamon, and a secret blend of several liqueurs. They don't share the recipe (believe us, we've tried!), but we think we have managed to re-create the flavor in this pie. We named this pie after Nicolé, the image captured in one of three huge art nouveau stained-glass windows in the restaurant and who can bear witness to the innumerable meals—and cocktails—we have enjoyed there.

1. MAKE THE FILLING: Sprinkle the gelatin over 2 tablespoons of the coffee in a small bowl and set aside.

2. In a medium saucepan, combine the remaining coffee, the sugar, and salt. Cook over medium heat until the sugar is dissolved, about 3 minutes. Reduce the heat to medium-low, add the chocolate chips, and continue to cook until the chips are completely melted, about 5 minutes. Remove the saucepan from the heat and stir in the gelatin mixture, mixing until the gelatin is melted, about 1 minute.

3. Strain the mixture through a fine-mesh sieve into a large heat-safe bowl to ensure no unmelted chunks of chocolate or gelatin make it into the pie. Stir in the Amaretto, Grand Marnier, Frangelico, Bailey's, Galliano, and Kahlúa. Allow the mixture to cool to room temperature, about 20 minutes, stirring occasionally. The mixture should be slightly thickened but not set.

INGREDIENT	VOLUME	WEIGHT (STANDARD)	WEIGHT (METRIC)
FILLING			
Unflavored powdered gelatin	1½ teaspoons		
Strong brewed coffee or espresso, cooled	½ cup	4 ounces	113 grams
Sugar	¼ cup	1.75 ounces	50 grams
Salt	¼ teaspoon		
Milk chocolate baking chips	½ cup	3 ounces	85 grams
Amaretto liqueur	4 teaspoons	0.6 ounce	18 grams
Grand Marnier liqueur	4 teaspoons	0.65 ounce	19 grams
Frangelico liqueur	4 teaspoons	0.65 ounce	19 grams
Baileys Irish Cream liqueur	4 teaspoons	0.75 ounce	21 grams
Galliano liqueur	4 teaspoons	0.65 ounce	19 grams
Kahlúa liqueur	4 teaspoons	0.8 ounce	23 grams
Heavy cream	1 cup	8.2 ounces	232 grams
TOPPING			
Cappuccino Whipped Cream (page 258)	1 recipe		

4 FILL THE CRUST: Using an electric mixer, whip the cream until it holds stiff peaks, 1 to 3 minutes. With the mixer on low speed, drizzle the coffee mixture into the whipped cream. Continue to beat on low speed until the mixture is uniform. Pour into the prepared crust and smooth the top. Refrigerate until set, at least 3 hours.

5 ADD THE TOPPING: Using a small offset spatula, spread Cappuccino Whipped Cream across the surface of the set pie. The goal here is to just make sure the whole surface is covered, reserving as much of the whipped cream as possible for decorating. Transfer the remaining whipped ream to the prepared piping bag (we like a medium St. Honoré tip for its peaked shape). Decoratively cover the surface of the pie with the remaining whipped cream. Serve immediately. (Refrigerate leftovers for up to 3 days.)

SHERRY RAISIN

MAKES ONE 9-INCH PIE

WHAT YOU NEED

- Pie dough for a Standard Single Crust (page 35)
- 9-inch standard pie plate
- Pie crust shield or foil (see page 19)
- Instant-read thermometer
- Piping bag (see page 21) fitted with a Wilton #1M or other large piping tip (optional)

This pie is our modern take on rum-raisin pie. Don't get us wrong—we love our rum, but sherry and raisins go together like rainbows and unicorns. If you're not familiar, cream sherry is a sweet fortified wine from Spain that pairs very well with dried fruits, especially raisins. In this pie, sherry is used in three ways: to soak the raisins, to flavor the custard, and to enhance the whipped cream. Obviously, a small glass of sherry, especially a sweet Pedro Ximénez, would pair very well with this pie.

1. PARTIALLY BLIND-BAKE THE CRUST: Follow the instructions on page 47. The pie will bake longer after the filling is added, so it should not be completely browned at this point. Remove the pie dish from the oven, set it on a wire cooling rack, and remove the foil or parchment and pie weights. Reduce the oven temperature to 300°F.

2. MAKE THE FILLING: While the crust is baking, combine the raisins and 2 tablespoons of the cream sherry in a food processor. Process the raisin mixture until the raisins are ground and the mixture just begins to form a paste. Transfer the raisins to a small bowl and cover with plastic wrap.

3. When the crust has about 15 minutes left to bake, start the sherry-raisin custard. In a large microwave-safe bowl, whisk together the remaining 2 teaspoons sherry, the melted butter, granulated sugar, brown sugar, cinnamon, and salt until the mixture is uniform, about 1 minute. (Here and in the remaining step for making the custard,

recipe continues

INGREDIENT	VOLUME	WEIGHT (STANDARD)	WEIGHT (METRIC)
SHERRY RAISIN CUSTARD			
Raisins	1¼ cups	6.25 ounces	177 grams
Cream sherry (see headnote)	2 tablespoons plus 2 teaspoons	1.3 ounces	37 grams
Unsalted butter, melted	8 tablespoons	4 ounces	113 grams
Granulated sugar	½ cup	3.5 ounces	100 grams
Light brown sugar, lightly packed	½ cup	3.5 ounces	100 grams
Ground cinnamon	½ teaspoon		
Salt	½ teaspoon		
Egg, at room temperature	1 large		
Egg yolks, at room temperature	3 large		
Sour cream, at room temperature	Scant 1 cup	8 ounces	227 grams
All-purpose flour	3 tablespoons	0.95 ounce	27 grams
Heavy cream, at room temperature	½ cup	4.1 ounces	116 grams
TOPPING			
Sherry Whipped Cream (page 258)	1 recipe		

do not over-whisk the mixture or you will incorporate unnecessary air into the custard.) Whisk in the egg and egg yolks until they are fully incorporated. Whisk in the sour cream and then whisk in the flour until incorporated. Scrape the sides of the bowl, and whisk in the heavy cream just until uniform and no streaks are visible. Set the mixture aside until the pie crust is finished blind-baking.

4. Remove the hot crust from the oven. Keep the oven temperature at 300°F.

5. Heat the custard mixture in the microwave on medium (50%) power until the mixture reaches 130°F on an instant-read thermometer, 3 to 5 minutes, stirring every 30 seconds or so.

6. Using an offset spatula, press the raisin paste into an even layer on the bottom of the hot crust. If the crust shifts around in the pan, gently hold the crust in place by pressing with the back of a spoon on a spot already covered with the raisin paste.

7. FILL THE CRUST AND BAKE: Place a pie crust shield on the pie. Slowly transfer the warm custard to the hot crust, trying not to dislodge the raisin paste (pouring it over the back of a spoon helps). Carefully return the filled crust to the oven (the crust will be quite full) and bake until the edges of the pie are puffed and set, and an approximately 4-inch circle in the center of the pie is still jiggly, 35 to 40 minutes (the center of the pie will be 170°F on an instant-read thermometer).

8. Cool the pie on a wire rack until it reaches room temperature, about 4 hours. Once the pie has cooled, refrigerate the pie until cold and set, at least 4 hours (or up to 2 days).

9. ADD THE TOPPING: Before serving, spread the Sherry Whipped Cream over the top of the pie. Alternatively, you can pipe the topping decoratively using the prepared piping bag. (Store any leftovers in the refrigerator for up to 2 days.)

Variation:
ELDERFLOWER RAISIN

Follow the directions for the Sherry Raisin pie, but substitute equal amounts of golden raisins for the dark raisins, elderflower liqueur for the cream sherry, and ground ginger for the ground cinnamon. This pie's flavor is more delicate than the Sherry Raisin, but there's no doubt that it's equally delicious, especially if you're a fan of elderflower liqueur. St-Germain is our favorite.

Old Fashioned CHERRY

MAKES ONE 9-INCH PIE

WHAT YOU NEED
- Pie dough for a Standard Single Crust (page 35)
- 9-inch standard pie plate
- Immersion circulator with water bath
- Vacuum sealer
- Pie crust shield or foil (see page 19)

Bet you thought that a pie called "old fashioned" might actually be a fairly traditional recipe. Nope. The name here refers to the cocktail made with bourbon, muddled orange peel, and cherries. In fact, there is nothing old-fashioned about this pie. After extracting the flavor from the oils in the zest, the filling is cooked sous vide, ensuring perfectly cooked cherries infused with the flavors of bourbon and orange. The pie is topped with a streusel made from breakfast cereal—adding a malty flavor that pairs so well with the bourbon.

1. MAKE THE PUFFED WHEAT STREUSEL: Pulse the flour, sugar, salt, and butter in the bowl of a food processor until evenly mixed and moistened. Add the cereal and pulse a few more times to incorporate the cereal pieces. Scrape the mixture onto a 13 by 9-inch sheet pan lined with parchment or wax paper. Break apart any large clumps and pinch together some of the smaller bits into ¼- to ½-inch nuggets. Place the pan in the freezer until ready to use. (Cover the pan with foil to store the nuggets for a few days in the freezer.)

2. MAKE THE FILLING: Place the granulated sugar in a small bowl with the orange zest. Break up all the clumps of zest into the sugar by rubbing them between your thumb and fingertips in the bowl until

recipe continues

INGREDIENT	VOLUME	WEIGHT (STANDARD)	WEIGHT (METRIC)
PUFFED WHEAT STREUSEL (can be prepared a few days in advance)			
All-purpose flour	½ cup	2.5 ounces	71 grams
Light brown sugar, lightly packed	¼ cup	1.75 ounces	50 grams
Salt	⅛ teaspoon		
Unsalted butter, melted	6 tablespoons	3 ounces	85 grams
Sweetened puffed wheat cereal, such as Golden Crisp	1 cup	1.25 ounces	35 grams
FILLING			
Granulated sugar	1 scant cup	6.7 ounces	190 grams
Finely grated orange zest	2 tablespoons		
Finely ground quick-cooking tapioca, such as Minute	3 tablespoons	1.05 ounces	30 grams
Salt	⅛ teaspoon		
Frozen sweet cherries	¾ cup	3 ounces	85 grams
Orange juice	1 tablespoon	0.5 ounce	14 grams
Almond extract	¼ teaspoon		
Bourbon	¼ cup	1.75 ounces	50 grams
Frozen sour or tart cherries	3½ cups	21 ounces	600 grams
Dried sour cherries	⅔ cup	3 ounces	85 grams

uniformly incorporated and the sugar is orange. This releases the oils of the zest into the sugar.

3. Set up the water bath for your immersion circulator and start heating the water to 150°F (see the sous vide instructions on page 28). Adjust the oven racks to the middle and bottom positions and preheat the oven to 350°F.

4. Put the orange-sugar, tapioca, and salt into a vacuum-sealable bag and shake them around until well mixed. Roughly chop the frozen sweet cherries into ¼-inch dice and add them to the bag with the sugar. Now add the orange juice, almond extract, bourbon, frozen sour cherries, and dried sour cherries. Gently shake the bag to disperse the contents and then vacuum-seal it. Cook the cherries sous vide in the water bath for 1 hour.

5. PARTIALLY BLIND-BAKE THE CRUST: Follow the instructions on page 47. The pie will bake longer after the filling is added, so it should not be completely browned at this point. Remove the pie dish from the oven, set it on a wire cooling rack, and remove the foil or parchment and pie weights. Keep the oven at 350°F.

6. FILL THE CRUST: Remove the cherry bag from the water bath and dry it off with a kitchen towel. Place a pie crust shield on the pie to prevent splashes. Cut open the bag and pour the filling into the warm crust, using a bench scraper to get everything out of the bag. The filling will look quite loose at this point. Don't worry—it will thicken up. Keep the shield on and bake on the bottom rack of the oven for 10 minutes.

7. After 10 minutes of baking, evenly sprinkle the frozen topping nuggets over the pie surface. Keep the pie shield on and bake until the topping has browned slightly and the filling is just starting to bubble at the edge, about 25 minutes. Remove the pie from the oven, place on a cooling rack, and allow the pie to cool completely, at least 4 hours, before serving. (Leftovers can be stored, covered, at room temperature for up to 3 days.)

MANGO
Colada

MAKES ONE 9-INCH PIE
WHAT YOU NEED
- Pie dough for a Standard Single Crust (page 35)
- 9-inch standard pie plate
- Pie crust shield or foil (see page 19)
- Instant-read thermometer

This pie embraces the beauty of the mango as a take on the classic piña colada drink. A creamy mango custard is crowned with a generous layer of coconut rum–scented whipped cream, crisp coconut chips, and cubes of fresh, juicy mango. Baked coconut chips can usually be found in the produce section of the grocery store. If you want, you can substitute toasted sweetened coconut flakes for the chips, but the crunch won't be the same. You can puree your own extra-ripe mangos, but they can be fibrous; we recommend frozen mango puree, often found in the international section of the freezer aisle.

1. PARTIALLY BLIND-BAKE THE CRUST: Follow the instructions on page 47. The pie will bake longer after the filling is added, so it should not be completely browned at this point. Remove the pie dish from the oven, set it on a wire cooling rack, and remove the foil or parchment and pie weights. Reduce the oven temperature to 300°F.

2. MAKE THE CUSTARD: While the crust is baking, place the mango puree, sugar, and salt in a large microwave-safe bowl. Whisk in the eggs one at a time, followed by the sour cream and mango rum, until the mixture is uniform throughout. Set aside until the pie crust is finished blind-baking.

3. Once the crust is removed from the oven, heat the mango mixture in the microwave on medium (50%) power until the mixture reaches 130°F on an instant-read thermometer, 3 to 5 minutes, stirring every 30 seconds or so.

4. FILL THE CRUST AND BAKE: Place a pie crust shield on the crust. Transfer the warmed custard mixture to the warm pie crust and bake until the edges are set and the center 3 inches of the pie jiggle when the pie is gently shaken (the custard will be 180°F on an instant-read thermometer), 15 to 20 minutes.

INGREDIENT	VOLUME	WEIGHT (STANDARD)	WEIGHT (METRIC)
MANGO CUSTARD			
Mango puree, frozen and thawed (see headnote)	¾ cup	7.5 ounces	213 grams
Sugar	¾ cup	5.25 ounces	150 grams
Salt	¼ teaspoon		
Eggs	4 large		
Sour cream	½ cup	4.25 ounces	121 grams
Mango-flavored rum, such as Cruzan	1½ teaspoons		
TOPPING			
Coconut Whipped Cream (page 258)	1 recipe		
Toasted coconut chips (see page 28)	½ cup	1 ounce	28 grams
Mango, cut into ¼-inch cubes (optional)	¼ cup	1.5 ounces	43 grams

5. Cool the pie on a wire rack until it reaches room temperature, about 4 hours. Once the pie has cooled, refrigerate the pie until cold and set, at least 3 more hours or up to overnight.

6. PREPARE THE TOPPING: Spread the Coconut Whipped Cream across the top of the pie, leaving ½ inch of the orange custard visible at the edges. Sprinkle the coconut chips and cubed mango, if using, over the top of the pie just before serving. (Refrigerate leftovers for up to 2 days; the coconut chips might be softer on the second day; to retain crispness, sprinkle the chips over a slice just before serving instead of topping the whole pie all at once.)

BELLINI

MAKES ONE 9½-INCH DEEP-DISH PIE

WHAT YOU NEED

• Deep-Dish Single Crust (page 36), baked and cooled in a 9½-inch deep-dish pie pan
• Instant-read thermometer

The Bellini, our favorite brunch cocktail, was our inspiration for this pie. Echoing the flavors of this fruity and fizzy standard of midday drinking, the layers of peach chiffon and Champagne mousse are a perfect treat to cap any meal of the day! This recipe uses just over 1 cup of Champagne, and what you do with the rest is none of our business.

1. MAKE THE PEACH CHIFFON: In a medium bowl, whip the cream on medium-high speed until it holds stiff peaks, 1 to 3 minutes. Put the whipped cream in the refrigerator while preparing the rest of the filling.

2. In a food processor, puree the sliced peaches until they are smooth. You will need 1⅓ cups of puree.

3. In a large microwave-safe bowl, sprinkle the gelatin over ½ cup of the peach puree. Set aside to soften for 5 minutes. Microwave the gelatin mixture on high (100%) power for about 30 seconds, stirring every 10 seconds, until the mixture is just bubbling at the edges and the gelatin seems dissolved (it's hard to tell because the puree is not a clear liquid, but if the puree has begun to bubble at the edges, it should be fine). Add the remaining peach puree to the gelatin mixture and stir to combine. Stir in the salt, lemon juice, and peach schnapps; set aside until the mixture is no longer warm, stirring occasionally to prevent the mixture from setting prematurely.

recipe continues

INGREDIENT	VOLUME	WEIGHT (STANDARD)	WEIGHT (METRIC)
PEACH CHIFFON			
Heavy cream	⅔ cup	5.45 ounces	155 grams
Peeled peach slices, fresh or thawed frozen	2 cups	12 ounces	340 grams
Unflavored powdered gelatin	1 tablespoon	0.3 ounce	9 grams
Salt	pinch		
Fresh lemon juice	2 teaspoons		
Peach schnapps liqueur	1 tablespoon	0.55 ounce	15 grams
Egg whites	2 large		
Sugar	⅔ cup	4.65 ounces	133 grams
CHAMPAGNE MOUSSE			
Demi-sec Champagne or another sweet sparkling white wine	1 cup plus 2 tablespoons	9 ounces	255 grams
Unflavored powdered gelatin	1¾ teaspoons		
Egg yolks	3 large		
Sugar	¼ cup	1.75 ounces	50 grams
Salt	pinch		
Heavy cream	¾ cup	6.15 ounces	174 grams

4. While the peach mixture is cooling, bring approximately 1 inch of water to a simmer in a large saucepan. In a large heat-safe bowl (preferably the metal bowl of an electric stand mixer), whisk together the egg whites and sugar. Heat the egg-white mixture over the simmering water until the mixture is quite hot (160°F on an instant-read thermometer) and the sugar is completely dissolved.

5. Beat the hot egg-white mixture on medium-high speed (and with the whisk attachment if using a stand mixer) until it holds soft peaks and has completely cooled (the outside of the bowl should not feel warm), 5 to 10 minutes, depending on the power of your mixer and the temperature of your kitchen.

6. Fold the whipped egg-white mixture into the peach mixture until it is mostly incorporated. Fold in the cold whipped cream until the mixture is uniform and no white streaks of egg white or whipped cream remain. Transfer the mixture to the cooled pie crust and refrigerate until the mixture is cold and firm, at least 4 hours (or up to overnight).

7. MAKE THE CHAMPAGNE MOUSSE: Place 2 tablespoons/1 ounce/ 28 grams of the Champagne in a small microwave-safe bowl. Sprinkle the gelatin over the top and set aside.

8. In a medium saucepan, whisk together the egg yolks, sugar, salt, and remaining 1 cup/8 ounces/227 grams of the Champagne in a medium saucepan. Over medium-low heat, cook the mixture, stirring constantly, until it reaches 160°F on an instant-read thermometer and thickens and coats the back of a spoon, 3 to 5 minutes (the mixture will become foamy). Remove from the heat and continue whisking for about 2 minutes, until it cools slightly.

9. Microwave the gelatin mixture at high (100%) power, stirring every 5 seconds until it just begins to bubble at the edges and the gelatin is dissolved, about 15 seconds. Whisk the gelatin into the hot Champagne-egg mixture. Strain through a fine-mesh sieve into a large bowl, and then set the mixture aside to cool for 10 minutes, stirring occasionally to prevent it from setting.

10. In a large bowl, use a hand mixer on medium-high to whip the cream until it holds stiff peaks, 1 to 3 minutes. Reduce the speed to low and drizzle in the cooled Champagne mixture, whipping on low until no streaks remain. Spread the Champagne mousse over the peach chiffon filling and refrigerate the pie until it is cold and set, about 4 hours (or up to overnight), before serving. (Store any leftovers in the refrigerator.) The pie is best eaten within 2 days.

BLUE RIBBON BONUS:

Tiny Bubbles

For the ultimate Champagne fizz, sprinkle one recipe of Pie-Proof Popping Sugar (page 263) over the top of the peach layer before it cools and sets, and before adding the Champagne mousse.

HAIR
of the **DOG**

MAKES ONE 9-INCH PIE

WHAT YOU NEED
- Pie dough for a Standard Single Crust (page 35)
- 9-inch standard pie plate
- Instant-read thermometer
- Pie crust shield or foil (see page 19)

Some say that having just a bit more alcohol—in other words, the hair of the dog that bit you—the morning after a night of excessive drinking can take the edge off that crummy feeling. This unlikely combination of tomato, vodka, celery salt, and just a bit of sugar creates a Bloody Mary custard that is a dead ringer for your favorite morning cocktail. The hot sauce glaze gives a spicy pop to each bite and the Cheetos-coated crust provides a fun crunch. Whether it will cure you of your hangover, who can say? We're not providing medical advice here, just making pie.

1. MAKE THE CRUST: Place the Cheetos in the bowl of a food processor and process until finely ground. Roll out the dough (see page 42) to a ⅛-inch thickness. Sprinkle half the Cheetos crumbs across the surface of the dough. Press them into the dough by rolling the rolling pin across the surface once or twice. Flip the dough over and repeat the process with the other half of the Cheetos crumbs. Now lift and fit the dough into a standard 9-inch pie plate. Crimp the edges as desired (see page 24). Place the prepared crust in the freezer to chill until quite firm, about 20 minutes. Preheat the oven to 350°F.

recipe continues

INGREDIENT	VOLUME	WEIGHT (STANDARD)	WEIGHT (METRIC)
CRUST ADDITION			
Cheetos Crunchy Cheese Flavored Snacks	1½ cups	3.5 ounces	100 grams
FILLING			
Sugar	¾ cup	5.25 ounces	150 grams
Xanthan gum (see Sources, page 265)	⅛ teaspoon		
Celery salt	¼ teaspoon		
Ground black pepper	⅛ teaspoon		
Ground cayenne	⅛ teaspoon		
Eggs	4 large		
Tomato paste	½ cup	4.7 ounces	132 grams
Sour cream	½ cup	4.25 ounces	121 grams
Vodka	¼ cup	1.9 ounces	55 grams
Worcestershire sauce	1 teaspoon		
TOPPING			
Xanthan gum (see Sources, page 265)	⅛ teaspoon		
Sugar	1 teaspoon		
Hot sauce	2 tablespoons	1 ounce	28 grams
Tomato paste	1 tablespoon	0.6 ounce	17 grams

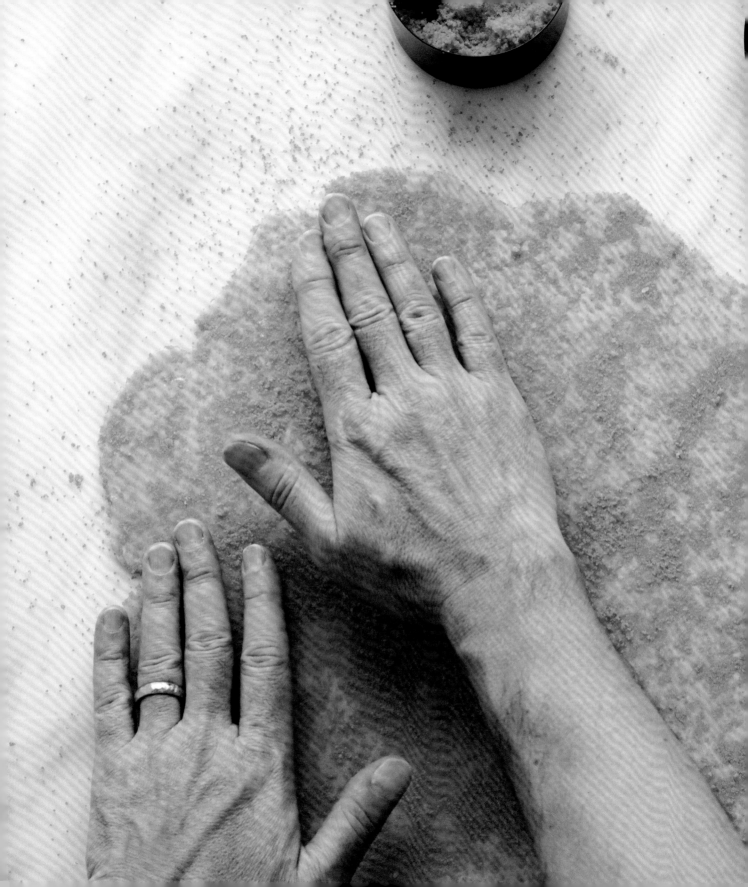

2. PARTIALLY BLIND-BAKE THE CRUST: Follow the instructions on page 47. The pie will bake longer after the filling is added, so it should not be completely browned at this point. Remove the pie dish from the oven, set it on a wire cooling rack, and remove the foil or parchment and pie weights. Reduce the oven temperature to 300°F.

3. PREPARE THE FILLING: In a small bowl, whisk together the sugar, xanthan gum, celery salt, black pepper, and cayenne.

4. In a medium microwave-safe bowl, whisk the eggs together. Add the tomato paste, sour cream, vodka, and Worcestershire sauce, and whisk until uniformly incorporated. Add the sugar mixture and whisk until uniformly combined. Microwave the filling mixture on medium (50%) power for about 45 seconds, stir, and check the temperature. Repeat this step until the mixture reaches 130°F, about 4 minutes total, depending on the power of your microwave.

5. FILL THE CRUST: Place a shield on the crust to protect the edges from drips and splashes, and pour the mixture into the warm pie shell. Transfer the filled pie to the oven and bake until the filling has puffed and set, about 30 minutes. If the center still sloshes when the pie is moved, continue baking, checking every 5 minutes until the filling has puffed and the center wobbles slightly. Set the pie aside at room temperature to cool completely.

6. MAKE THE TOPPING: Whisk the xanthan gum and sugar in a small bowl. Add the hot sauce and tomato paste, and whisk until well mixed. Pour the hot sauce glaze into a small squeeze bottle and drizzle decoratively over the surface of the pie. The pie can be served immediately. (Refrigerate leftovers for up to 1 day.)

CHEESE COURSE

MAKES ONE 9½-INCH DEEP-DISH PIE

WHAT YOU NEED

- Nut Graham Cracker Crust (page 50), made with walnuts and baked and cooled in a 9½-inch deep-dish pie plate with no lip
- Pie crust shield or foil (see page 19)
- Piping bag (see page 21) fitted with a Wilton #1M or other large star piping tip (optional)

We are always making little notes about inspirations for new pies. These lists grow and change over time, with some ideas getting overlooked and bypassed repeatedly. Such was the case with figs for us. Every time we would eat figs, or see them at the market, we'd be reminded of that longstanding plan to develop a fun fig pie. Part of the problem is that there are so many different directions to go with figs. Fresh versus dried? Light with citrus and honey or dark with warm winter spices? We finally had that moment of illumination: figs and gorgonzola cheese—like a cheese course after dinner, but as an actual dessert. The addition of port and toasted walnuts rounds out this classic combination in a new, exciting, and sophisticated way.

1. **MAKE THE FILLING:** In a medium saucepan, stir together the figs, port, honey, salt, and 1 cup/8.35 ounces/236 grams of water and bring to a simmer over medium heat. We really like weighing sticky ingredients like the honey directly into the saucepan (another benefit of using a scale!), but feel free to use a measuring cup if you prefer. As the figs start to soften, press on them with a rubber spatula as you stir the pot. After about 15 to 20 minutes, the figs will have mostly broken down and the mixture will have thickened to a jam-like consistency.

2. **FILL THE CRUST:** Place a pie crust shield on the crust to protect the edges from drips and splashes, and spread the mixture in the pie crust. Allow the pie to cool completely to room temperature and then refrigerate it until cold, at least 2 hours.

3. **PREPARE THE TOPPING:** Place the cream in a medium microwave-safe bowl. Microwave the cream until it is just starting to boil, 1 to 2 minutes, depending on the power of your microwave oven. Stir in the sugar until dissolved, then stir in the gorgonzola. The cheese crumbles will mostly melt, leaving a few streaks of visible cheese. Cover with plastic wrap and place the bowl in the refrigerator until cold, at least 2 hours.

INGREDIENT	VOLUME	WEIGHT (STANDARD)	WEIGHT (METRIC)
FILLING			
Dried figs, stemmed and quartered	3 cups	14.5 ounces	411 grams
Ruby port wine	1 cup	8 ounces	227 grams
Honey	¼ cup	3 ounces	85 grams
Salt	pinch		
TOPPING			
Heavy cream	1 cup	8.2 ounces	232 grams
Sugar	⅓ cup	2.35 ounces	67 grams
Gorgonzola dolce blue cheese, crumbled	½ cup	2 ounces	57 grams
Mascarpone cheese	1 cup	8 ounces	227 grams
Walnuts, chopped and toasted	½ cup	2 ounces	57 grams

4. Add the mascarpone to the cold cheese mixture. Using a hand mixer or whisk, beat on medium-high speed until it holds stiff peaks, about 2 minutes. Spread this topping onto the chilled pie and smooth with an offset spatula. Alternatively, you can pipe the topping decoratively using the prepared piping bag.

5. Sprinkle the toasted walnut pieces decoratively around the edge of the pie. Keep the pie refrigerated until serving. (Refrigerate leftovers for up to 3 days.)

The NEW CUSTARD PIES

These custard pies are creamy egg-based delights that are baked in their pie crusts and served cold. These are traditionally home-style pies such as Thanksgiving pumpkin and Key lime pie. We added some bold new flavors and used innovative techniques to ensure that these sometimes finicky custards bake perfectly from edge to edge.

Dulce de
PUMPKIN

MAKES ONE 9½-INCH DEEP-DISH PIE

WHAT YOU NEED
- Pie dough for Deep-Dish Single Crust (page 36)
- 9½-inch deep-dish pie plate
- Vanilla or Caramel Whipped Cream (optional; page 257), for serving

This is a pumpkin pie for people who think they don't like pumpkin pie. We improve on the classic pumpkin pie with a boost of caramel flavor in the filling and a slathering of dulce de leche, topped with toffee bits for a welcome crunch. This creation will turn even the staunchest squash skeptic into a bona fide believer in the power of pumpkin pie.

1. PARTIALLY BLIND-BAKE THE CRUST: Follow the instructions on page 47. The pie will bake longer after the filling is added, so it should not be completely browned at this point. Keep the oven at 350°F.

2. MAKE THE PUMPKIN FILLING: While the crust is baking, in a large mixing bowl, whisk together the pumpkin puree and eggs. Whisk in the caramel-flavored condensed milk, cinnamon, nutmeg, ginger, cloves, salt, and vanilla.

3. FILL THE CRUST AND BAKE: Remove the pie crust from the oven and remove the pie weights and lining. Re-whisk the pumpkin mixture to ensure nothing has settled in the bottom of the bowl and then pour the pumpkin mixture into the hot crust. Continue to bake until the edges of the pie are set and the center 4 inches of the pie are still jiggly when jostled, 30 to 40 minutes. Remove the pie from the oven and set aside to cool to room temperature, then refrigerate to chill completely, at least 4 hours and up to 1 day before adding the topping. The pie will firm up as it chills.

INGREDIENT	VOLUME	WEIGHT (STANDARD)	WEIGHT (METRIC)
PUMPKIN FILLING			
Canned pumpkin puree (not pumpkin pie filling)	1 15-ounce can	15 ounces	425 grams
Eggs	2 large		
Caramel-flavored sweetened condensed milk	1 14-ounce can	14 ounces	397 grams
Ground cinnamon	1¼ teaspoons		
Ground nutmeg	½ teaspoon		
Ground ginger	½ teaspoon		
Ground cloves	⅛ teaspoon		
Salt	pinch		
Vanilla extract	2 teaspoons		
TOPPING			
Dulce de leche	1 cup	10.7 ounces	304 grams
Toffee bits (see opposite)	½ cup	2.8 ounces	80 grams

4. MAKE THE TOPPING: Gently warm the dulce de leche until it's soft and spreadable like peanut butter (about 15 seconds on medium [50%] power in the microwave should do it). Smooth the dulce de leche evenly over the top of the cold pie. Return the pie to the refrigerator until you are ready to serve it.

5. Just before serving, sprinkle the toffee bits over the dulce de leche, slice, and serve with Vanilla or Caramel Whipped Cream, if desired. (Refrigerate leftovers for up to 2 days; after the first day, the toffee bits will soften and begin to dissolve.)

THE GUYS TALK PIES: *Toffee Bits*

What exactly are toffee bits? Are they like a Heath Bar? Sort of. In the chocolate chip section at the grocery store, there's usually a spot reserved for "toffee bits." We prefer the plain toffee bits (sometimes labeled as Heath Bits 'O Brickle) for this recipe, rather than the ones covered in chocolate, but if you can find only chocolate-covered bits, those will work. Your pie will be a bit sweeter, that's all. You can also crush some store-bought plain English toffee to make your own bits.

UN-BEET-ABLE

MAKES ONE 9-INCH PIE

WHAT YOU NEED

- Pie dough for a Standard Single Crust (page 36)
- 9-inch standard pie plate
- Pie crust shield or foil (see page 19)
- Instant-read thermometer

We know that a "beet pie" may sound a little too earthy, but we make pies out of sweet potatoes and pumpkins all the time, and no one bats an eye! The beet, like the sweet potato, is just another root vegetable—but then, it's not *just another root vegetable*. In this pie, the honorable beet is transformed into a delicious, delicately spiced pie with a creamy, bright pink filling. The pie is topped with a goat cheese frosting, our take on the cream cheese frostings that pair so well with carrot cake (another root vegetable, by the way). If goat cheese isn't your thing, you can substitute an equal amount of cream cheese. If you don't want to cook your own beets, you can substitute 10½ ounces of roasted vacuum-sealed beets if your grocery store's produce section has them.

1. PARTIALLY BLIND-BAKE THE CRUST: Follow the instructions on page 47. The pie will bake longer after the filling is added, so it should not be completely browned at this point. Remove the pie dish from the oven, set it on a wire cooling rack, and remove the foil or parchment and pie weights. Keep the oven at 350°F.

2. MAKE THE BEET CUSTARD FILLING: While the crust is baking, poke the beets all over with a fork and place them on a microwave-safe plate. Cook the beets on high (100%) power for 15 to 20 minutes, turning the beets over every 5 minutes. The beets are done when a sharp knife can be easily inserted and removed from the beets without resistance. (We recommend covering the beets with a few paper towels so they don't splatter the interior of your microwave while cooking.)

3. Set the beets aside until they are cool enough to handle, 10 to 20 minutes. Peel the beets using a vegetable peeler. (Consider wearing gloves for this unless you want bright pink fingers.) Cut the peeled beets into 1-inch chunks, and measure out about 1⅔ cups/10½ ounces/ 298 grams. Use the remaining beets in a salad.

recipe continues

INGREDIENT	VOLUME	WEIGHT (STANDARD)	WEIGHT (METRIC)
BEET CUSTARD FILLING			
Red beets, raw, washed, greens removed	about 3 medium	1½ pounds	680 grams
Granulated sugar	½ cup	3.5 ounces	100 grams
Light brown sugar, lightly packed	½ cup	3.5 ounces	100 grams
Whole milk	½ cup	4.25 ounces	121 grams
Heavy cream	¾ cup	6.15 ounces	174 grams
Eggs	2 large		
Egg yolk	1 large		
Ground cinnamon	½ teaspoon		
Ground ginger	¼ teaspoon		
Ground cloves	⅛ teaspoon		
Salt	¼ teaspoon		
Vanilla extract	½ teaspoon		

INGREDIENT	VOLUME	WEIGHT (STANDARD)	WEIGHT (METRIC)
GOAT CHEESE FROSTING			
Goat cheese (chèvre), at room temperature	1 cup	4 ounces	113 grams
Unsalted butter, at room temperature	2 tablespoons	1 ounce	28 grams
Confectioners' sugar	¾ cup	3 ounces	85 grams
Vanilla extract	½ teaspoon		

4. Add the beet chunks, the granulated sugar, and brown sugar to the bowl of a food processor. Process until the mixture is completely smooth, scraping the sides as necessary. Add the milk and cream, and process until incorporated, and then pulse in the eggs and egg yolk, followed by the cinnamon, ginger, cloves, salt, and vanilla. Scrape the sides of the food processor bowl and process for 10 seconds to ensure that all the ingredients are incorporated. Place a pie crust shield on the pie and pour the processed beet mixture into the hot crust.

5. BAKE THE PIE: Bake until the edges are puffed and the filling jiggles just slightly when bumped and the center of the pie reads 165°F on an instant-read thermometer, 35 to 45 minutes. Remove from the oven and cool the pie to room temperature, about 3 hours, then refrigerate the pie for at least 4 hours (or up to overnight).

6. MAKE THE GOAT CHEESE FROSTING: Blend the goat cheese and butter together with a hand mixer in a medium bowl until creamy, about 2 minutes on medium-high speed. Add the confectioners' sugar and vanilla, and mix on medium-low speed to combine, then increase the speed to medium-high until the mixture is light and creamy, about 5 minutes. Spread the frosting over the top of the chilled pie and serve. (Refrigerate leftovers for up to 2 days.)

ROASTING BEETS

If you like, you can roast the beets in an oven instead of the microwave. Unless you have two ovens, roast the beets before the pie crust is baked. Preheat the oven to 375°F. Wrap each beet in a sheet of aluminum foil sprayed with cooking spray or otherwise lightly greased. Bake the beets for 50 to 60 minutes, or until a sharp knife can be easily inserted and removed from the beets without resistance. When the beets are cooked through, remove from the oven, and carefully open the foil so the beets can start to cool. Continue with Step 2 of the recipe. Remember to return the oven temperature to 350°F!